QUICK FROM SCRATCH
Soups & Salads

Chicken Noodle Soup with Parsnips and Dill, page 63

QUICK FROM SCRATCH
Soups & Salads

American Express Publishing Corporation
New York

Editor in Chief: Judith Hill

Art Director: Nina Scerbo
Designer: Leslie Andersen
Photographer: Melanie Acevedo
Food Stylists: Roscoe Betsill,
Bettina Fisher, and A.J. Battifarano
Prop Stylist: Robyn Glaser
Wine Editor: Steve Miller

Managing Editor: Terri Mauro
Associate Editor: Laura Byrne Russell
Copy and Production Editor: Amy Schuler
Copy Editor: Barbara A. Mateer
Contributing Editor: Catherine Young
Editorial Assistant: Evette Manners
Portrait Photographer: Chris Dinerman

Production Manager: Stuart Handelman

Senior Vice President/Chief Marketing Officer: Mark V. Stanich
Vice President, Books and Products: Marshall A. Corey
Marketing Manager: Bruce Spanier
Senior Fulfillment Manager: Phil Black
Business Manager: Doreen Camardi
Marketing Coordinator: Richard Nogueira

Cover Design: Perri DeFino and Elizabeth Rendfleisch
Recipe Pictured on Front Cover: Tomato Soup with Chickpeas and Past, page 35

AMERICAN EXPRESS PUBLISHING CORPORATION
© 1998, 2002, 2004 American Express Publishing Corporation

LIBRARY OF CONGRESS CATALOGING-IN-PUBLICATION DATA AVAILABLE

ISBN 0-916103-90-0

Published by American Express Publishing Corporation
1120 Avenue of the Americas, New York, NY 10036

Printed in China.

CONTENTS

RECIPES PICTURED ABOVE: (*left to right*) pages 33, 89, 77

Tasting salads while developing this book.

Judith Hill is the editor in chief of FOOD & WINE Books, a division of American Express Publishing. Previously she was editor in chief of COOK'S Magazine, director of publications for La Varenne École de Cuisine in Paris, from which she earned a Grand Diplôme, and an English instructor for the University of Maryland International Division in Germany. Her book credits include editing cookbooks for Fredy Girardet, Jane Grigson, Michel Guérard, and Anne Willan.

Laura Byrne Russell earned a bachelor's degree in finance and worked in stock and bond sales for a few years before deciding that food is more fun. She went back to school, this time to The Culinary School at Kendall College in Illinois. After gaining experience in professional kitchens in Chicago and New York City, she came to FOOD & WINE Books, where she works as both an editor and a recipe developer.

SOUPS AND SALADS FOR ALL SEASONS

Soups are for winter, salads for summer, right? Well, not exactly. Not in my house, anyway. And restaurants, ever vigilant to excise any item that doesn't sell, certainly keep both soups and salads on the menu all year.

I love a big salad for dinner whether it's January or July. Try our **Salmon-and-Potato Cakes with Mixed Greens** (page 105), **Curly-Endive Salad with Bacon and Poached Eggs** (page 121), or **Warm Sausage-and-Potato Salad** (page 161), and I think you'll agree.

Laura Russell, who was the developer and tester for most of the recipes in this book, is more of a soup person. She makes **Tortellini and Spinach in Garlic Broth** (page 19), **Tomato Soup with Chickpeas and Pasta** (page 35), or **Smoked-Trout Chowder** (page 43) regardless of the weather.

In fact, nearly all the recipes in this collection are seasonless. Only a few salads, like those that rely on perfectly red-ripe tomatoes, need be reserved for summer. And just a handful of the heartiest soups, such as **Smoked-Sausage, Cabbage, and Potato Soup** (page 85) or **Black-Bean and Corned-Beef Soup** (page 91), really spell cold-weather-in-a-cozy-kitchen.

Of course, it's up to you, but we hope you'll mix and match recipes and seasons. The wonderful thing about all the dishes here is that they're quick, delectable, and, along with some good bread, meals in themselves. And that's a great thing anytime of year.

Judith Hill
Editor in Chief
FOOD & WINE Books

Before You Begin

You'll find test-kitchen tips and ideas for ingredient substitutions presented with the individual recipes throughout *Quick from Scratch: Soups & Salads*. In this opening section, we've gathered thoughts and tips that apply to all, or at least a substantial number, of the recipes. These are the facts and opinions that we'd like you to know before you use the recipes and keep in mind as you cook. In addition to ingredient information and test-kitchen tips, you'll find a chart characterizing different types of salad greens, and our wine editor's thoughts on serving wine with soups and salads.

RECIPES PICTURED OPPOSITE: (top) pages 101, 65, 51; (center) pages 37, 107, 95; (bottom) pages 163, 71, 167

ESSENTIAL INGREDIENT INFORMATION

Broth, Chicken

We tested the recipes in this book using canned low-sodium chicken broth. You can almost always substitute regular for low-sodium broth; just cut back on the salt in the recipe. And if you keep home-made stock in your freezer, by all means feel free to use it. We aren't suggesting that it won't work as well, only that we know the dishes taste delicious even when made with canned broth.

Butter

Our recipes don't specify whether to use salted or unsalted butter. We generally use unsalted, but in these savory dishes, it really won't make a big difference which type you use.

Cheese, Grated

We frequently call for Parmesan cheese in our recipes. Not only is it widely available, but fresh-grated Parmigiano-Reggiano is hard to beat. However, Parmesan has become something of a generic term including all Italian grating cheeses, and we use it in that sense. Feel free to substitute Romano or Asiago.

Citrus Juice

Many of our recipes call for lemon or lime juice. For a bright boost of flavor, use juice from fresh fruit. The bottled stuff just doesn't taste as good.

Garlic

The size of garlic cloves varies tremendously. When we call for one minced or chopped clove, we expect you to get about three quarters of a teaspoon.

Ginger, Fresh

Fresh ginger, or gingerroot, is a knobby, tan-skinned rhizome found in the produce section of your supermarket. You need to peel its thin skin before using; this is most easily accomplished by scraping it with a spoon. After peeling, the ginger is ready to be grated, sliced, or chopped.

Mustard

When we call for mustard, we mean Dijon or a similar good-quality type. We never, ever mean yellow ballpark mustard.

Oil

Cooking oil in these recipes refers to readily available, reasonably priced nut, seed, or vegetable oil with a high smoking point, such as peanut, sunflower, canola, safflower, or corn oil. These can be heated to about 400° before they begin to smoke, break down, and develop an unpleasant flavor.

Nuts

Our quick pantry wouldn't be complete without several kinds of nuts. Keep in mind that nuts have a high percentage of oil and can turn rancid quickly. We store ours in the freezer to keep them fresh.

Parsley

Many of our recipes call for chopped fresh parsley. The flat-leaf variety has a stronger flavor than the curly, and we use it most of the time, but unless the type is specified, you can use either.

Pepper

■ There's nothing like fresh-ground pepper. If you've been using preground, buy a pepper mill, fill it, and give it a grind. You'll never look back.

■ To measure your just-ground pepper more easily, become familiar with your own mill; each produces a different amount per turn. You'll probably find that ten to fifteen grinds produces one-quarter teaspoon of pepper, and then you can count on that forever after.

Tomatoes, Canned

In some recipes, we call for "crushed tomatoes in thick puree." Depending on the brand, this mix of crushed tomatoes and tomato puree may be labeled crushed tomatoes with puree, with added puree, in tomato puree, thick style, or in thick puree. You can use any of these.

Wine, Dry White

Leftover wine is ideal for cooking. It seems a shame to open a fresh bottle for just a few spoonfuls. Another solution is to keep dry vermouth on hand; you can use whatever quantity is needed and the rest will keep indefinitely.

Zest

Citrus zest—the colored part of the peel, without any of the white pith—adds tremendous flavor to many a dish. Remove the zest from the fruit using either a grater or a zester. A zester is a small, inexpensive, and extremely handy tool. It has little holes that remove just the zest in fine ribbons. A zester is quick, easy to clean, and never scrapes your knuckles.

Faster, Better, Easier
TEST-KITCHEN TIPS

Fresh ingredients

The soup pot is not a place to hide less-than-fresh ingredients. You don't have to choose your most gorgeous specimens to simmer in the soup, but don't add anything that's over the hill, either. The final flavor won't lie.

Improving canned broth

In a perfect world, we'd all keep gallons of homemade chicken stock on hand for last-minute use. Fortunately, since that may be unrealistic, canned low-sodium chicken broth makes a reliable alternative. Simmering the soup for at least fifteen minutes gives the flavors of the other ingredients a chance to blend with and improve the taste of the broth. For our quicker-cooking soups, we often include other liquids, such as water or wine, to mute the canned taste.

Pureeing soups

For perfectly smooth soups, we think a standing or immersion blender is the best tool. You can also get great results using a food processor or a food mill, but the blender produces pureed soups with an especially silky texture. Be careful when pureeing hot liquids in the blender, though. Hold a kitchen towel over the lid while the motor's running to catch any escaping molten liquid.

Starchy soup ingredients

The longer pasta, potatoes, and rice sit in soup the more liquid they absorb, which makes them mushy and the soup too thick. If you plan to make soup ahead of time, cook starchy ingredients in a separate pot of water, store them separately, and stir them into the soup while you're reheating it. Or, wait and cook starchy ingredients directly in the soup as it's reheating.

Leftover soup

■ The flavor of soup actually improves after a day or two. Save leftovers by pouring the soup into an airtight container and storing it in the refrigerator.

■ Another great time-saver is to freeze leftover soup in single-serving or family-size containers. Use the soup within about three months.

■ If leftover soup has thickened too much, stir in a little broth or water to thin it to the consistency you like. Taste the soup before serving and add salt and pepper if needed.

■ Serve leftover pureed vegetable soup chilled for a refreshing summer dish. Be aware, though, that you'll probably need to add more salt and pepper, since cold deadens flavor.

Washing, drying, and storing salad greens

■ Salad greens can harbor so much dirt and sand that a simple rinsing isn't enough. To **clean** them properly, remove any wilted or brown outer leaves and tear the remaining leaves into bite-size pieces. Fill the sink or a large bowl with water. Immerse the greens in the water, swish them around, and let the sediment sink to the bottom. Lift the greens from the water leaving the dirt behind, dump or drain the water, rinse the sink or bowl, and repeat until the greens are perfectly clean. This process may seem troublesome, but it's well worth the effort to avoid grittiness.

■ **Dry** the greens by giving them a whirl in a salad spinner, or drain them in a colander and then on paper towels or a clean kitchen towel. Greens intended for salads need to be especially dry, or the dressing won't cling.

■ To **store** washed greens for a few hours, put them in a bowl, cover with a moist paper towel, and refrigerate. For longer storage, wrap the washed and dried greens in paper towels, put in a perforated plastic bag, and store in the refrigerator's vegetable drawer. Depending on the type, the greens should stay fresh for four to five days.

Measuring greens

The easiest way to measure greens for salads is in a large (two quart) measuring cup. Put the trimmed greens in the measuring cup and tamp them down very lightly. The greens should be loosely packed for an accurate measurement.

Full-flavored salads

It's not just wet greens than can ruin a salad; all salad ingredients—especially rice, pasta, cooked vegetables—should be thoroughly drained. Otherwise the dressing, and consequently the flavor, will be diluted.

Salad bowls

Salad dressings often include acidic ingredients, and so we call for tossing salads in a glass or stainless-steel bowl. What we are really asking for is a nonreactive bowl, so go ahead and use a wood, plastic, or even ceramic one. Just don't use aluminum.

Tossing salads

Start by using a large bowl so that you'll have plenty of room to toss the ingredients. Put the greens and dressing in this bowl. Often you can make the dressing in the large bowl and add the greens to it, thus using only one bowl rather than two. Using your hands or wooden spoons, toss until all the greens are lightly coated. Taste for salt and pepper and add as needed. Always toss your salad just before serving so the greens don't wilt into a soggy mess.

SALAD GREENS (AND REDS)

Each type of green provides its own distinctive texture and flavor. For the most part, the sturdier the texture and the stronger the flavor, the heavier and bolder-tasting dressing the lettuce can accommodate. Toss delicate Bibb lettuce with a light herb vinaigrette, but if it's a blue-cheese-dressing night, romaine will be a better choice. Not that you *have* to use a heavy dressing with sturdy greens—a simple, classic vinaigrette (see page 180) is good with anything.

Name of Green	TEXTURE	FLAVOR	SUBSTITUTE	DRESSING Flavor	Texture
ARUGULA (rocket)	tender	sharp, spicy	watercress	mild to medium	light
BELGIAN ENDIVE	tender, crisp	slightly bitter	radicchio	mild to strong	light to heavy
BIBB	tender, soft	delicate, mild	Boston	mild	light
BOSTON	tender, soft	delicate, mild	Bibb	mild	light
CABBAGE, GREEN or RED	crisp, sturdy	strong	napa or Savoy cabbage	mild to strong	light to heavy
CURLY ENDIVE (chicory)	sturdy	bitter	radicchio	mild to strong	light to moderate
ESCAROLE	sturdy	moderate	romaine	mild to strong	light to heavy
ICEBERG	crisp	bland	romaine	mild to strong	light
LEAF, GREEN or RED	soft	mild	mixed greens (mesclun)	mild	light
MIXED GREENS (mesclun)	varies	balanced	red and green leaf	mild to medium	light
RADICCHIO	sturdy	bitter	Belgian endive	mild to strong	light to moderate
ROMAINE	crisp	mild	escarole	mild to strong	light to heavy
SPINACH	tender	moderate	green or red leaf, watercress	mild to medium	light
WATERCRESS	tender	peppery	arugula	mild to strong	light

PAIRING WINE WITH SOUPS AND SALADS

Soups and salads, both simple, casual fare, are among today's favorite foods. But when we think of enjoying a relaxing glass of wine with either, most of us balk. Instinctively, we find the combination odd. There are, in fact, good reasons for this reaction and both soups and salads do present significant challenges to the would-be wine-and-food marriage broker. However, every challenge is also an opportunity, and to overlook the many wonderful wines that work splendidly with these dishes is to miss out on some very rewarding culinary synergy.

With soup, the issue is liquid with liquid; our gut tells us it won't work. Yet it does, and once you make the counterintuitive leap, the wine possibilities become almost endless. The main point to keep in mind is that soup flavors can be concentrated and intense, and in order to achieve a successful wine pairing, the wine should always be fuller-bodied and richer than the soup. Therefore, in the recommendations here, you will see chardonnay, pinot gris, and gewürztraminer among whites, and fairly big red wines such as syrah and zinfandel.

Most salads are finished with dressings that contain vinegar or lemon juice, the high acidity of which can eviscerate all but the crispest wines. No matter—there are many racy, light-bodied, refreshing wines that are ideally suited to salads. Excellent choices include rieslings of all kinds, sauvignon blanc, and chenin blanc; most Italian whites, such as pinot grigio, Soave, Orvieto, and vernaccia; and even some light reds such as Beaujolais and pinot noir. You will see these wines suggested again and again throughout this book.

I encourage you to try my recommendations. But keeping in mind the general guidelines here, you can feel free to experiment. You'll quickly discover which combinations you like best.

Steve Miller
Wine Editor

CHAPTER ONE

Vegetable & Legume Soups

TORTELLINI AND SPINACH IN GARLIC BROTH

Don't be tempted to cook the tortellini in the soup; they will soak up too much of that irresistibly garlicky broth. Cook them separately, as the soup simmers, and stir them in at the last moment.

WINE RECOMMENDATION
Tocai friulano, one of Italy's hidden treasures, bears no relation to the Tokays of Hungary or Alsace. It has a full body and penetrating citrus and nut flavors that will be superb here.

SERVES 4

2 tablespoons olive oil

5 cloves garlic, minced

3 cups water

3 cups canned low-sodium chicken broth or homemade stock

1½ teaspoons salt

1 pound fresh or frozen cheese tortellini

1 pound spinach, stems removed, leaves washed well (about 2¼ quarts)

Grated Parmesan, for sprinkling

1. In a large pot, heat the oil over moderately low heat. Add the garlic and cook, stirring, for 1 minute. Add the water, broth, and salt and bring to a boil. Reduce the heat and simmer, covered, for 10 minutes.

2. Meanwhile, in a large pot of boiling, salted water, cook the tortellini until just done, about 4 minutes for fresh or 12 minutes for frozen. Drain.

3. Add the spinach to the soup and cook until just wilted, about 1 minute. Stir in the tortellini. Serve the soup sprinkled with grated Parmesan and pass more of the grated cheese at the table.

VARIATIONS

■ Substitute one quart of shredded **escarole** for the spinach.

■ Use meat- or cheese-filled **ravioli** instead of the tortellini.

CREAMY ASPARAGUS SOUP WITH MUSHROOMS AND GRUYÈRE CROÛTES

A little white rice is all it takes to make this soup thick and creamy. The trick is in pureeing the soup so that the rice becomes silky smooth. We like to use a blender for the job; you may prefer a food processor.

WINE RECOMMENDATION

The wines of southern Italy, long ignored by wine lovers, are now recognized as among the most interesting the country has to offer. A full-bodied wine such as a white Greco di Tufo, an earthy, honeyed delight, will be terrific here.

SERVES 4

6½ tablespoons olive oil

10 ounces shiitake mushrooms, stems removed and caps sliced thin, or ½ pound regular white mushrooms including the stems, sliced

2¼ teaspoons salt

¼ teaspoon fresh-ground black pepper

1 large onion, chopped

1 quart water

1 quart canned low-sodium chicken broth or homemade stock

⅓ cup long-grain rice

2 pounds asparagus, tough ends snapped off and discarded, spears cut into 1-inch pieces

16 ½-inch slices baguette

¼ pound Gruyère, shredded

1. In a large pot, heat 2 tablespoons of the oil over moderately high heat. Add the mushrooms, ¼ teaspoon of the salt, and the pepper and cook, stirring occasionally, until the mushrooms are golden, about 5 minutes. Remove the mushrooms from the pot and set aside. Reduce the heat to moderately low and add another 1½ tablespoons of the oil to the pot. Add the onion and cook, stirring occasionally, until translucent, about 5 minutes.

2. Add the water, broth, rice, and the remaining 2 teaspoons of salt to the pot. Bring to a boil. Continue boiling for 10 minutes, stirring occasionally. Add the asparagus. Cook until the asparagus is tender, about 5 minutes.

3. In a blender or food processor, puree the soup until completely smooth. Return the soup to the pot and stir in the reserved mushrooms.

4. Meanwhile, heat the broiler. Put the bread on a baking sheet and brush both sides of the bread with the remaining 3 tablespoons of oil. Broil the bread until brown, about 2 minutes. Turn and top with the Gruyère. Broil until the cheese melts, about 2 minutes longer.

5. Reheat the soup if necessary. Serve topped with the Gruyère croûtes.

POTATO-AND-BROCCOLI SOUP

Bright green broccoli florets float prettily in this hearty soup, but it's broccoli stems that do the real work. They're cooked with the potatoes and then pureed to form a creamy base. A final touch of Parmesan gives the soup an Italian feel.

WINE RECOMMENDATION
Pinot grigio is the all-purpose Italian white. Its full body matches the creaminess of this soup, while its high acidity offers contrast. The relatively neutral taste of the wine allows the soup's subtle flavors to come through. No wonder pinot grigio is so popular.

SERVES 4

- 2 tablespoons butter
- 1 onion, chopped
- 2 cloves garlic, minced
- 1¾ pounds broccoli, thick stems peeled and diced (about 2 cups), tops cut into small florets (about 1 quart)
- 1½ pounds boiling potatoes (about 5), peeled and cut into ½-inch cubes
- 3 cups canned low-sodium chicken broth or homemade stock
- 3 cups water
- 1¾ teaspoons salt
- ¼ teaspoon fresh-ground black pepper
- ½ cup grated Parmesan

1. In a large pot, melt the butter over moderately low heat. Add the onion; cook, stirring occasionally, until translucent, about 5 minutes.

2. Add the garlic, broccoli stems, potatoes, broth, water, salt, and pepper. Bring to a boil. Reduce the heat and simmer until the vegetables are almost tender, about 10 minutes.

3. In a food processor or blender, pulse the soup to a coarse puree. Return the soup to the pot and bring to a simmer. Add the broccoli florets and simmer until they are tender, about 5 minutes. Stir ¼ cup of the grated Parmesan into the soup, and serve the soup topped with the remaining cheese.

VARIATION

If you'd prefer a completely **smooth soup**, add the broccoli florets to the pot after the potatoes have cooked for five minutes, and continue simmering until all of the vegetables are tender, about five minutes more. Puree the soup until smooth. This would also make a great first course for six people.

INDIAN SPLIT-PEA AND VEGETABLE SOUP

Carrots, white potatoes, and spinach are our vegetables of choice here, but you could try green beans, zucchini, cauliflower, or sweet potatoes. Another option: Pass some plain yogurt at the table to stir into each serving for a touch of tang.

WINE RECOMMENDATION
A simple, straightforward, fruity Beaujolais will make a fine accompaniment to this soup. Its vivid cherry and berry flavors will contrast and highlight, not compete with, the earthiness of the dish.

SERVES 4

1   10-ounce package frozen chopped spinach

1   cup yellow or green split peas

9   cups water, more if needed

2   1-inch pieces fresh ginger, peeled, 1 piece chopped

1¾ teaspoons salt

2   tablespoons butter

1   jalapeño pepper, seeds and ribs removed, minced

¼   teaspoon turmeric

1   tablespoon ground coriander

1½ teaspoons ground cumin

4   carrots, cut into ¼-inch slices

1   pound boiling potatoes (about 3), peeled and cut into ½-inch cubes

1. Remove the spinach from the freezer. In a medium saucepan, combine the split peas, 3 cups of the water, the unchopped piece of ginger, and ½ teaspoon of the salt. Bring to a boil. Reduce the heat and simmer, covered, stirring frequently, until the split peas are tender, about 30 minutes. Add more water if necessary to keep the peas from sticking to the pan.

2. Meanwhile, in a large pot, melt the butter over moderately low heat. Stir in the chopped ginger, the jalapeño, turmeric, coriander, cumin, carrots, potatoes, and the remaining 1¼ teaspoons salt. Add the remaining 6 cups water. Bring to a boil. Reduce the heat and simmer, stirring occasionally, until the vegetables are almost tender, about 10 minutes. Stir in the spinach and simmer 5 minutes longer.

3. Remove the whole piece of ginger from the cooked split peas and then stir the split peas into the soup. Simmer the soup for 5 minutes, stirring occasionally.

LENTIL SOUP WITH CAULIFLOWER AND BACON

Since the cauliflower only cooks in the soup for a short period of time, the vegetable doesn't develop that overwhelming flavor often associated with it. The flavor of bacon, though, comes through loud and clear.

WINE RECOMMENDATION
Look to South Africa's native pinotage grape for something a little unusual to accompany this savory soup. Pinotage produces supple, spicy red wines with a smoky tang and a delicious berry fruitiness.

SERVES 4

  6   slices bacon, cut crosswise into thin strips
  1   onion, chopped
  1   cup lentils
  2   teaspoons salt
 ¼ teaspoon fresh-ground black pepper
1½ teaspoons dried rosemary, crumbled
  1   bay leaf
  9   cups water
  1   small head cauliflower (about 1½ pounds), cut into small florets (about 1 quart)
 ⅓ cup chopped fresh parsley

1. In a large pot, cook the bacon strips until crisp. Remove the bacon with a slotted spoon and drain on paper towels. Discard all but 2 tablespoons of the bacon fat or, if there's less than 2 tablespoons, add enough olive oil to make up the amount.

2. Reduce the heat to moderately low. Add the onion to the pot and cook, stirring occasionally, until translucent, about 5 minutes.

3. Add the lentils, salt, pepper, rosemary, bay leaf, and water to the pot. Bring to a boil. Reduce the heat and simmer, partially covered, stirring occasionally, for 15 minutes. Add the cauliflower florets and simmer, stirring occasionally, until the cauliflower and lentils are tender, about 15 minutes longer. Remove the bay leaf.

4. Stir the parsley into the soup. Serve the soup topped with the bacon.

VARIATION

Substitute **broccoli** florets for the cauliflower. Add them after the lentils have cooked for about twenty-five minutes and then simmer until the broccoli is tender, five to ten minutes longer.

LENTIL AND LINGUINE SOUP

As they cook, the lentils and linguine slurp up much of the vegetable-flavored broth, leaving a thick and hearty soup. Of course, if the soup is *too* thick for your taste, just stir in a little extra water.

WINE RECOMMENDATION
The soup's flavors are firmly grounded in the soil and will be well served by a wine whose profile is earthy as well. Try a white Côtes-du-Rhône; while it's a bit more difficult to find than the red variety, you'll be surprised by how well it works here.

SERVES 4

- 3 tablespoons olive oil
- 1 large onion, chopped
- 2 cloves garlic, minced
- 3 carrots, chopped
- 1 cup lentils
- 2½ quarts water, more if needed
- 2 teaspoons salt
- 1 bay leaf
- Pinch red-pepper flakes (optional)
- ¼ pound linguine, broken into 1½-inch pieces
- ¼ teaspoon fresh-ground black pepper
- ½ cup chopped fresh parsley
- ¼ cup grated Parmesan

1. In a large pot, heat the oil over moderate heat. Add the onion, garlic, and carrots and cook, stirring occasionally, until the vegetables start to soften, about 10 minutes.

2. Add the lentils, water, salt, bay leaf, and red-pepper flakes to the pot. Bring to a boil. Reduce the heat and simmer, partially covered, stirring occasionally, for 15 minutes. Add the linguine and simmer, stirring occasionally, until the lentils are tender and the pasta is done, 15 to 20 minutes longer.

3. Stir the black pepper and the parsley into the soup. Top each serving with some of the grated Parmesan.

VARIATIONS

- Substitute one chopped **fennel** bulb for the carrots.

- Stir one-and-a-half cups of **spinach**, cut into very thin strips, into the soup along with the parsley.

CHICKPEA AND LENTIL SOUP

Harira is our favorite Moroccan soup, but we rarely have the hours it takes to simmer the lamb that's traditionally a part of it. With some trepidation, we developed this vegetarian version—and it knocked our socks off. Top each serving with a squeeze of lemon juice and a sprinkling of chopped dates for a real Moroccan feel.

WINE RECOMMENDATION

What a combination this dish and gewürz-traminer will make. The wine's full body will stand up to the soup, and the complex interplay of spices between the wine and soup will keep you fascinated. The wine can be from Washington or Alsace, but it should be dry.

SERVES 4

  2 tablespoons butter

  1 onion, chopped

  2 ribs celery, chopped

$^1/_2$ teaspoon ground ginger

$^1/_4$ teaspoon turmeric

$^1/_8$ teaspoon ground cinnamon

1$^3/_4$ teaspoons salt

$^1/_4$ teaspoon fresh-ground black pepper

  1 cup lentils

6$^1/_2$ cups water

1$^3/_4$ cups canned crushed tomatoes in thick puree (one 15-ounce can)

1$^2/_3$ cups drained and rinsed canned chickpeas (one 15-ounce can)

$^1/_3$ cup chopped cilantro or parsley

1. In a large pot, melt the butter over moderately low heat. Add the onion and celery and cook, stirring occasionally, until the vegetables start to soften, about 10 minutes. Stir in the ginger, turmeric, cinnamon, salt, pepper, and lentils.

2. Add the water and tomatoes to the pot. Bring to a boil. Reduce the heat and simmer, partially covered, stirring occasionally, until the lentils are tender, 25 to 30 minutes. Add the chickpeas and simmer 5 minutes longer. Stir in the cilantro or parsley.

VARIATIONS

■ Add one-and-a-half cups of diced left-over cooked **lamb** with the chickpeas.

■ Add two cups of shredded **cabbage** and an additional half cup of water along with the tomatoes.

■ Use **saffron** instead of the turmeric.

CHICKPEA AND ROMAINE SOUP WITH GOLDEN VERMICELLI

In Spain, this soup would be made with *fideos*, a type of thin pasta. We've used vermicelli instead, but the complex taste of the golden broth, rich with paprika and turmeric, makes the soup's Spanish origins apparent nonetheless.

WINE RECOMMENDATION

Since the inspiration for this soup comes from Spain, why not the wine as well? A Rioja Crianza will be perfect here. *Crianza* means aged for less time than the more complex Reserva and Gran Reserva, and so the wine will be fresh and fruity.

SERVES 4

   4   tablespoons olive oil

   1   onion, chopped

   1   clove garlic, minced

   ¼   teaspoon turmeric

   ½   teaspoon paprika

   ¼   teaspoon cayenne

   2   plum tomatoes, chopped

   2   cups drained and rinsed canned chickpeas (one 19-ounce can)

   3   cups canned low-sodium chicken broth or homemade stock

   3   cups water

   1   teaspoon salt

   ¼   pound vermicelli, broken in half

   ½   head romaine lettuce (about ⅔ pounds), shredded (about 5 cups)

1. In a large pot, heat 2 tablespoons of the oil over moderately low heat. Add the onion, garlic, turmeric, paprika, and cayenne and cook, stirring occasionally, until the onion is translucent, about 5 minutes. Stir in the tomatoes and cook 5 minutes longer.

2. Add the chickpeas, broth, water, and salt. Bring to a boil and then reduce to a simmer.

3. Meanwhile, in a large frying pan, heat the remaining 2 tablespoons of oil over moderate heat. Add the vermicelli and cook, stirring occasionally, until golden, about 5 minutes. Remove the browned pasta with a slotted spoon; add it to the soup along with the romaine. Simmer until the pasta is tender, about 5 minutes.

VARIATIONS

We originally made this soup with **Swiss chard**. When it came time to retest, we were out of chard but had plenty of romaine; we used that and liked the soup even better. Swiss chard still makes a fine substitution, though, as does **spinach**.

Tomato Soup with Chickpeas and Pasta

Canned tomatoes—not the seasonally sensitive fresh ones—provide the flavor here, so you can whip up this heartwarming soup any time of year. If you'd like to use an herb other than sage, either rosemary or marjoram would be a good choice.

WINE RECOMMENDATION

Italians have had two millennia to develop an incredible synergy between their wines and tomato-based cuisine. Take advantage of this experience and pair this soup with a cherry- and herb-scented Chianti Classico or Rufina.

SERVES 4

  7 cups canned tomatoes with their juice (two 28-ounce cans)

  2 tablespoons olive oil

  1 onion, chopped

  2 cloves garlic, minced

1½ teaspoons dried sage

  2 cups canned low-sodium chicken broth or homemade stock

  2 cups water

1¾ teaspoons salt

  ½ cup ditalini or other small pasta

  2 cups drained and rinsed canned chickpeas (one 19-ounce can)

  ⅓ cup chopped fresh parsley

  ¼ teaspoon fresh-ground black pepper

  ⅓ cup grated Parmesan, plus more for serving

1. In a food processor or blender, puree the tomatoes with their juice. Set aside.

2. In a large pot, heat the oil over moderately low heat. Add the onion and cook, stirring occasionally, until soft, about 10 minutes. Stir in the garlic.

3. Add the pureed tomatoes, the sage, broth, water, and salt to the pot. Bring to a boil. Stir in the pasta and chickpeas. Bring the soup back to a boil, then reduce the heat. Cook, partially covered, stirring occasionally, until the pasta is tender, about 15 minutes. Stir in the parsley, pepper, and the ⅓ cup grated Parmesan. Serve topped with additional Parmesan.

TEST-KITCHEN TIP

Look for high-quality canned tomatoes for this soup, such as plum tomatoes from the San Marzano region of Italy.

BLACK-EYED-PEA SOUP WITH GREENS AND HAM

There's nothing better than a pot of Southern-style slow-simmered greens, flavored with salty ham and a dose of vinegar. Our quick soup starts with the same ingredients, adds black-eyed peas and a shot of Tabasco, and cooks in no time. Add more Tabasco or vinegar to suit your taste.

WINE RECOMMENDATION

This soup has more than enough oomph to partner a rich California syrah. Spicy blackberry and green-olive flavors, a strong earthy streak, and solid structure are its hallmarks, and all of these will go well here.

SERVES 4

2 tablespoons cooking oil

6 scallions, white bulbs and green tops chopped and reserved separately

2 cloves garlic, minced

½ pound Swiss chard or other greens, tough stems removed, leaves washed well and shredded (about 4 cups)

2 10-ounce packages frozen black-eyed peas (about 4 cups)

3 cups water

3 cups canned low-sodium chicken broth or homemade stock

½ teaspoon Tabasco sauce

1¾ teaspoons salt

1 ½-pound piece ham, diced

¼ teaspoon fresh-ground black pepper

2 teaspoons red- or white-wine vinegar

1. In a large pot, heat the oil over moderately low heat. Add the scallion bulbs and garlic and cook, stirring occasionally, for 2 minutes.

2. Add the Swiss chard, black-eyed peas, water, broth, Tabasco, and salt to the pot. Bring to a boil. Reduce the heat and simmer, partially covered, stirring occasionally, until the black-eyed peas are tender, about 20 minutes.

3. Stir the ham into the soup and cook until the ham is warmed through, about 2 minutes. Remove the pot from the heat and stir in the pepper, vinegar, and scallion tops.

VARIATIONS

Instead of the Swiss chard, use your own favorite greens. **Collard, mustard, kale,** or **beet greens** would each lend its unique flavor to the soup.

CABBAGE-AND-WHITE-BEAN SOUP WITH PROSCIUTTO

Prosciutto beautifully complements cabbage and beans, but if you toss it into the soup pot its flavor cooks away to nothing. Sprinkle some over the top of each serving instead.

WINE RECOMMENDATION
There is a revolution going on in Italian wine, with more choices than ever available from the southern regions of the country. Try a Greco di Tufo, a rich, earthy, nutty white from Campania, for a perfect accompaniment to this rustic soup.

SERVES 4

2 tablespoons olive oil

3 cloves garlic, minced

6 fresh or canned plum tomatoes, chopped

½ small head Savoy cabbage (about ¾ pound), cut into 1-inch squares (about 5 cups)

1 quart water

2 cups canned low-sodium chicken broth or homemade stock

1 teaspoon dried rosemary, crumbled

1¼ teaspoons salt

2 cups drained and rinsed canned white beans, preferably cannellini (from one 19-ounce can)

¼ pound sliced prosciutto, chopped

1. In a large pot, heat the oil over moderately low heat. Add the garlic and tomatoes and cook, stirring frequently, for 5 minutes.

2. Add the cabbage, water, broth, rosemary, and salt. Bring to a boil. Reduce the heat and simmer, partially covered, until the cabbage is tender, about 20 minutes.

3. Stir in the beans and simmer until just warmed through, about 3 minutes. Ladle the soup into bowls and sprinkle the prosciutto over the top.

SAVOY CABBAGE

Beautiful crinkled leaves make Savoy cabbage the most attractive member of the cabbage family. It also has a unique flavor, mellower than other varieties, even a little bit sweet. But you can certainly substitute regular green cabbage here if you prefer.

Fish &
Shellfish Soups

SMOKED-TROUT CHOWDER

Smoked fish—already cooked and intensely flavorful—is an ideal addition to dishes when time is of the essence. We've used trout here, but another flaky fish, such as haddock or whitefish, would work just as well.

WINE RECOMMENDATION
California chardonnays can be overpowering, but this chowder provides a perfect showcase. Try a fruity chardonnay from Napa or the Sonoma Valley.

SERVES 4

1   tablespoon butter

2   ribs celery, chopped

6   scallions, white bulbs and green tops chopped and reserved separately

2   cloves garlic, minced

1   pound baking potatoes (about 2), peeled and cut into 1/2-inch cubes

1/4   cup dry white wine

2   cups water

1   quart canned low-sodium chicken broth or homemade stock

1   teaspoon dried thyme

1   bay leaf

1 1/4   teaspoons salt

1   cup half-and-half

2   fillets peppered smoked trout, skin removed, fish flaked

1. In a large pot, melt the butter over moderately low heat. Add the celery, the chopped scallion bulbs, and the garlic and cook, stirring occasionally, until the vegetables start to soften, about 10 minutes.

2. Add the potatoes, wine, water, broth, thyme, bay leaf, and salt to the pot. Bring to a boil. Reduce the heat and simmer, partially covered, until the potatoes are tender, about 15 minutes.

3. Stir the half-and-half into the soup. Simmer until the soup starts to thicken, 2 to 3 minutes. Remove the pot from the heat and stir in the trout and the scallion tops. Remove the bay leaf from the soup.

NO PEPPERED TROUT?

If peppered smoked trout isn't available, use regular smoked trout and one teaspoon fresh-ground black pepper instead.

Asian Salmon-and-Rice Soup

A quick-to-make meal-in-a-bowl, this soup is inspired by similar one-dish wonders popular in China, Thailand, and Japan. The rice is sometimes cooked for so long that it completely dissolves, making a smooth gruel. Our version doesn't go that far; we like the rice to be soft, but still retain its shape.

WINE RECOMMENDATION
Pairing this soup with wine may be a bit of a stretch. A lager beer is a much better choice. Best of all: small flasks of warm, tangy sake.

SERVES 4

¾ cup long-grain rice

1½ pounds salmon fillet, skin removed, fish cut into 8 pieces

2 tablespoons soy sauce

1 tablespoon Asian sesame oil

10 cilantro stems, chopped, plus 1 cup cilantro leaves for garnish

1½ tablespoons minced fresh ginger

1 teaspoon salt

2 cups canned low-sodium chicken broth or homemade stock

4 cups water

3 scallions including green tops, chopped

1. Bring a medium pot of salted water to a boil. Stir in the rice and boil until almost tender, about 10 minutes. Drain.

2. Coat the salmon with the soy sauce and sesame oil.

3. In a large pot, combine the cooked rice, the cilantro stems, the ginger, salt, broth, and water. Bring to a boil. Reduce the heat and simmer, covered, stirring occasionally, for 15 minutes.

4. Add the salmon to the pot. Simmer, covered, until the salmon is just done, about 5 minutes. Remove the cilantro stems. Serve the soup garnished with the cilantro leaves and scallions.

Long-Grain vs. Short-Grain

We used long-grain rice for our soup. In China and Japan, it would be made with short-grain, which is starchier and dissolves into the soup more readily. If you want to go the short-grain route, arborio is readily available.

SHRIMP AND COD WITH TARRAGON BROTH AND CROUTONS

We think the combination of shrimp and cod keeps things interesting, but you could easily make this soup with just one or the other; simply double the quantity of whichever you choose. Sautéing the croutons in oil keeps them from getting soggy in the soup. The clam juice here will not make the soup taste like clams, since the juice is diluted with water and juice from the tomatoes; it just punches up the fish flavor.

WINE RECOMMENDATION

Fish soup with an herb-infused broth makes us think of sunlit patios overlooking a shimmering Mediterannean. If you were in Nice, you'd be drinking a Provençal rosé. Why not here?

SERVES 4

2 tablespoons butter

1 onion, chopped

2 ribs celery, chopped

2 cloves garlic, minced

1 teaspoon salt

½ cup dry white wine

1¼ teaspoons dried tarragon

1 cup bottled clam juice

1⅔ cups canned diced tomatoes with their juice (one 15-ounce can)

3 cups water

2 cups ½-inch bread cubes cut from good-quality white bread

2½ tablespoons olive oil

  Fresh-ground black pepper

⅓ cup chopped fresh parsley

¾ pound boneless, skinless cod fillet, cut into approximately 1-by-½-inch strips

¾ pound medium shrimp, shelled and halved lengthwise

1. In a large pot, melt the butter over moderately low heat. Add the onion, celery, garlic, and ¾ teaspoon of the salt. Cook, stirring occasionally, until the vegetables start to soften, about 10 minutes. Add the wine, tarragon, clam juice, tomatoes, and water. Bring to a boil. Reduce the heat and simmer for 10 minutes.

2. Meanwhile, put a medium frying pan over moderately low heat. Toss the bread cubes with the oil and the remaining ¼ teaspoon salt; add them to the pan. Cook, stirring frequently, until crisp and golden brown, about 5 minutes. Remove from the heat and toss the croutons with ⅛ teaspoon pepper and 2 tablespoons of the parsley.

3. Stir the cod and shrimp into the soup. Cook, stirring occasionally, until the seafood is just done, 3 to 5 minutes. Stir in ¼ teaspoon pepper and the remaining parsley and serve the soup topped with the croutons.

GREEN GAZPACHO WITH SHRIMP

Before the Spanish arrived in Mexico in the 1500s, they had never even seen a tomato, much less cooked with one. The Old Country gazpacho got its color from cucumbers, and once you've tried it you'll understand why the green version is still preferred over the red in some quarters. If you're using this uncooked soup as a first course instead of a main dish, it will serve six.

WINE RECOMMENDATION

When the dish is sweet, the wine should be, too. A late-harvest riesling, thick, rich, and vibrant with citrus and apricot flavors, will be incredible with this gazpacho.

SERVES 4

- 1 small loaf country-style white bread, cut into 1-inch cubes (about 6 cups)
- 2 tablespoons white-wine vinegar
- 1½ cups water, more if needed
- 3 cucumbers, peeled, halved lengthwise, seeded, and chopped
- ½ onion, chopped
- 2 teaspoons sliced almonds
- 2 cloves garlic
- 2 cups seedless green grapes
- ½ cup plus 2 tablespoons olive oil
- 2 teaspoons salt
- 1 pound shrimp, shelled and halved lengthwise

1. In a medium glass or stainless-steel bowl, combine 3 cups of the bread cubes with the vinegar. Add the water; set aside 5 minutes to soften.

2. In a blender, combine the cucumbers, onion, almonds, 1 clove of the garlic, and 1 cup of the grapes. Add the soaked bread, the ½ cup olive oil, and 1 teaspoon of the salt. Puree until smooth. Put the soup in the refrigerator to chill for about 20 minutes, or up to several hours.

3. Meanwhile, in a large nonstick frying pan, heat the remaining 2 tablespoons of oil over moderately high heat. Add the shrimp and the remaining 1 clove garlic and 1 teaspoon salt. Cook, stirring frequently, until the shrimp are just done, 3 to 5 minutes. Remove the shrimp with a slotted spoon.

4. Reduce the heat to moderate and add the remaining 3 cups of bread cubes. Cook, stirring frequently, until the bread is crisp and golden, about 5 minutes.

5. Cut the remaining grapes in half. In a small bowl, stir together the halved grapes, the shrimp, and the croutons. Serve the gazpacho (thinned with a small amount of water if it's thicker than you like) topped with the warm or room-temperature shrimp-and-grape mixture.

Peruvian Shrimp-and-Corn Chowder

In Peru, small streams wend their way from the mountains to the coast, and the delicious shrimp that fill them are cooked with local corn, squash, and potatoes to make this South American chowder called *chupe*. Don't peel the shrimp before cooking them in Step 1: The shells will flavor the cooking oil, which in turn will flavor the soup. The corn is traditionally left on the cob, but if the prospect of eating it this way (it *is* messy) bothers you, use two cups of kernels instead.

WINE RECOMMENDATION

We recommend the wines of Alsace again and again because they are so versatile, enhancing so many types of food. Here a pinot gris, nutty and rich, will have the body and flavor to beautifully highlight the soup.

SERVES 4

3 tablespoons cooking oil

1 pound unpeeled medium shrimp

3 teaspoons salt

1 onion, chopped

¼ teaspoon cayenne

½ teaspoon paprika

¼ teaspoon ground cumin

Dash Tabasco sauce

1 small butternut squash (about 1½ pounds), peeled, halved lengthwise, seeded, and cut into 1-inch cubes

½ small head green cabbage (about 1¼ pounds), chopped (about 1 quart)

1 pound baking potatoes (about 2), peeled and cut into 1½-inch chunks

4 ears of corn, halved

2 quarts water

1 cup heavy cream

1 cup frozen peas (optional)

1. In a large pot, heat the oil over moderate heat. Add the shrimp and 1 teaspoon of the salt and cook, stirring frequently, until the shrimp are pink and firm, about 5 minutes. Remove with a slotted spoon. When the shrimp are cool enough to handle, peel them and set aside.

2. Add the onion, cayenne, paprika, cumin, and another teaspoon of the salt to the pot. Cook, stirring occasionally, until the onion is translucent, about 5 minutes. Add the Tabasco, squash, cabbage, potatoes, corn, and water to the pot. Cover and bring to a boil. Reduce the heat and simmer, partially covered, until the potatoes are tender, about 15 minutes.

3. Add the cream and simmer for 10 minutes. Stir in the peeled shrimp, the remaining teaspoon of salt, and the peas, if using. Cook until the shrimp are just heated through, about 2 minutes.

BRAZILIAN SHRIMP SOUP

Coconut milk's rich flavor will keep you coming back for more of this substantial soup.
A true Brazilian version would include slices of okra, but ours is already so satisfyingly
thick that we left it out.

WINE RECOMMENDATION
The sweet elements here call for a somewhat assertive sweetness in the wine as well. A Vouvray demi-sec, from France's Loire Valley, ought to strike just the right balance.

SERVES 4

2	tablespoons cooking oil
1	onion, chopped
1	green bell pepper, chopped
3	cloves garlic, minced
¾	cup long-grain rice
¼	teaspoon red-pepper flakes
1¾	teaspoons salt
1¾	cups canned crushed tomatoes in thick puree (from one 15-ounce can)
5	cups water
1	cup canned unsweetened coconut milk
1½	pounds medium shrimp, shelled and cut in half horizontally
¼	teaspoon fresh-ground black pepper
1	tablespoon lemon juice
½	cup chopped fresh parsley or cilantro

1. In a large pot, heat the oil over moderately low heat. Add the onion, bell pepper, and garlic and cook, stirring occasionally, until the vegetables start to soften, about 10 minutes.

2. Add the rice, red-pepper flakes, salt, tomatoes, and water to the pot. Bring to a boil and cook until the rice is almost tender, about 10 minutes.

3. Stir the coconut milk into the soup. Bring back to a simmer and then stir in the shrimp. Simmer, stirring occasionally, until the shrimp are just done, 3 to 5 minutes. Stir in the black pepper, lemon juice, and parsley.

VARIATION

Instead of the shrimp, use one pound of boneless, skinless **chicken** breasts (about three), cut crosswise into quarter-inch strips. Cook for the same amount of time.

CORN-AND-CRABMEAT SOUP

The combination of sweet summer corn and delicate crabmeat is hard to beat. If you're feeling flush, you can use more crab, up to double the quantity. Serve the soup with something simple, such as grilled bread, topped with thin-sliced prosciutto if you like.

WINE RECOMMENDATION
The complex flavors of crab blend beautifully with those of chardonnay. White burgundies, made from chardonnay, have a more mineral taste and are less fruity than their American counterparts. Choose a Mâcon-Villages or Saint-Véran for a great match here.

SERVES 4

    1   quart fresh corn kernels (cut from about 8 ears)
    1   quart canned low-sodium chicken broth or homemade stock
    2   tablespoons butter
    1   onion, chopped
    ¼   cup dry white wine
    1½ teaspoons salt
    1½ cups milk
    ½   pound lump crabmeat, picked free of shell
    ⅓   cup chopped fresh chives or scallion tops

1. In a blender or food processor, combine the corn kernels and 2 cups of the broth. Pulse to a coarse puree.

2. In a large pot, melt the butter over moderately low heat. Add the chopped onion and cook, stirring occasionally, until translucent, about 5 minutes.

3. Add the corn puree, the wine, the remaining 2 cups of broth, and the salt to the pot. Bring to a boil. Reduce the heat and simmer, stirring occasionally, until the corn is tender, 10 to 15 minutes. Add the milk and bring just to a simmer. Stir in the crabmeat and chives.

VARIATIONS

■ Puree four cups (two ten-ounce packages) of defrosted **frozen corn** kernels with the milk (not the broth). Since frozen corn is already cooked, stir the puree into the soup when the milk is added in Step 3, bring just to a simmer, and then stir in the crabmeat and chives.

■ Substitute half a pound of medium peeled **shrimp** for the crabmeat. Stir the shrimp in along with the milk and cook for three to five minutes.

MUSSEL SOUP

With garlic, fennel, tomatoes, and a bit of orange zest, this soup has a nice Provençal feeling. And with cultivated mussels, which barely need to be cleaned, it's a snap to prepare. If you can't find mussels, try a fairly firm white fish, such as cod, instead—the soup will be different, but equally good.

WINE RECOMMENDATION
In Provence, where fish soups are staples, they're washed down with bottles of the delicious local pink wines. Look to the mourvèdre-based rosés from Bandol for a perfect match.

SERVES 4

5   tablespoons olive oil
1   onion, chopped
1   clove garlic, minced
1   fennel bulb, chopped
1   rib celery, chopped
1   bay leaf
    Grated zest of ½ orange
¼   teaspoon turmeric
3   plum tomatoes, chopped
1   cup dry white wine
8   ½-inch slices baguette
3   pounds mussels, scrubbed and debearded
3   cups water
1   teaspoon salt
¼   teaspoon fresh-ground black pepper
¾   cup heavy cream
¼   pound prosciutto or other flavorful ham, chopped

1. In a large pot, heat 3 tablespoons of the oil over moderately low heat. Add the onion, garlic, fennel, celery, bay leaf, orange zest, and turmeric. Cook, covered, stirring occasionally, until the vegetables are soft, about 15 minutes. Stir in the tomatoes and wine and simmer for 5 minutes.

2. Meanwhile, heat the broiler. Put the bread slices on a baking sheet and brush both sides with the remaining 2 tablespoons of oil. Broil the bread, turning once, until golden brown, about 4 minutes in all.

3. Discard any mussels that are broken or do not clamp shut when tapped. Add the water, salt, pepper, and mussels to the pot. Cover and bring to a boil. Cook, shaking the pot occasionally, just until the mussels open, 3 to 5 minutes.

4. As the mussels open, remove them from the pot with a slotted spoon. When the mussels are cool enough to handle, remove them from their shells. Remove the bay leaf. Stir the cream into the soup and bring just to a simmer. Stir in the mussels and the prosciutto and serve topped with the toasted slices of baguette.

Poultry & Meat Soups

POACHED-CHICKEN SOUP

Whether you feel a cold coming on or simply need a little soothing, there's nothing like a hot bowl of chicken soup. Poaching in broth also happens to be a great way to cook chicken, ranking right up there with roasted and fried among our favorite methods. You can eat the broth as a first course and then the chicken and vegetables, as is traditional in France, or do what we do—eat them together in a shallow bowl and feel supremely comforted.

WINE RECOMMENDATION
Though they are America's favorite wines, chardonnays are often quite awkward with food. Here, however, a California chardonnay that is medium-bodied and not too oaky will be just the ticket.

SERVES 4

2 tablespoons cooking oil

1 onion, chopped

1 carrot, chopped

1 rib celery, chopped

2 teaspoons salt

1 chicken (3 to 3½ pounds), cut into 8 pieces, skin removed

4 small red potatoes (about 1 pound), peeled and quartered

2 medium turnips, peeled and cut into eighths

1 cup canned low-sodium chicken broth or homemade stock

1 teaspoon red- or white-wine vinegar

2 quarts water

1 sprig fresh thyme, or ¼ teaspoon dried thyme

1 bay leaf

½ teaspoon fresh-ground black pepper

1 cup chopped fresh parsley

1. In a large pot, heat the oil over moderate heat. Add the onion, carrot, celery, and 1 teaspoon of the salt and cook, stirring occasionally, until the vegetables start to soften, about 10 minutes.

2. Add the chicken, potatoes, turnips, broth, vinegar, water, thyme, bay leaf, and the remaining 1 teaspoon salt. Cover and bring to a boil.

3. Reduce the heat and simmer, partially covered, until the chicken is just done, about 10 minutes for the breasts and 15 minutes for the legs and thighs; remove each piece as it is done.

4. Continue simmering the soup until the potatoes and turnips are tender, about 5 minutes longer. Stir in the pepper and parsley. Remove the thyme sprig and bay leaf. To serve, divide the chicken pieces among four shallow bowls and ladle the broth and vegetables over them.

CHICKEN NOODLE SOUP WITH PARSNIPS AND DILL

Lots of carrots and parsnips give old-favorite chicken noodle soup a sweet savor. To balance this effect, use the optional parsley, which is just slightly bitter.

WINE RECOMMENDATION
In just fifteen years, sauvignon blancs from New Zealand have burst upon the scene and risen to the top of the sauvignon-blanc heap. Sample their ripe citrus and herb flavors and bracing crispness with this soup and you will know why.

SERVES 4

1½ quarts canned low-sodium chicken broth or homemade stock

1 onion, chopped

4 carrots, halved lengthwise and cut crosswise into 1-inch pieces

4 parsnips, halved lengthwise and cut crosswise into 1-inch pieces

1½ teaspoons salt

¼ teaspoon fresh-ground black pepper

1 pound boneless, skinless chicken breasts (about 3)

1 cup wide egg noodles (about 2 ounces)

¼ cup chopped fresh dill

¼ cup chopped fresh parsley (optional)

1. In a large pot, combine the broth, onion, carrots, parsnips, salt, and pepper and bring to a simmer. Add the chicken breasts to the pot and simmer until just done, about 10 minutes. Remove the chicken; bring the soup back to a simmer. When the chicken breasts are cool enough to handle, cut them into bite-size pieces.

2. Meanwhile, stir the noodles into the soup. Simmer until the vegetables are tender and the noodles are done, about 5 minutes. Return the chicken pieces to the pot and then stir in the dill and the parsley.

VARIATIONS

■ Skip the parsnips and raise the number of **carrots** to eight.

■ Add one diced **turnip** to the mix.

■ Use **bone-in chicken** breasts and cook them for an additional ten minutes. The extra time in the pot will give the soup even more flavor.

CHICKEN-AND-AVOCADO SOUP WITH FRIED TORTILLAS

Here's a silky soup that doesn't rely on cream for its creamy texture; pureed avocados do the job nicely. It doesn't rely on long cooking for its full flavor, either—the soup's in the pot for less than ten minutes.

WINE RECOMMENDATION
Rich avocados demand a full-bodied white wine. This is a great opportunity to drink one of those big, oaky California chardonnays that can overpower less flavorful foods.

SERVES 4

3½ tablespoons cooking oil

4 6-inch corn tortillas, halved and cut crosswise into ¼-inch strips

1 clove garlic

1 jalapeño chile, seeds and ribs removed

2 ripe avocados, preferably Haas, skin and pit removed

1 tablespoon lime juice

¼ teaspoon Tabasco sauce, plus more to taste

3½ cups water

1½ teaspoons salt

¼ teaspoon fresh-ground black pepper

1 onion, chopped

3 cups canned low-sodium chicken broth or homemade stock

1 pound boneless, skinless chicken breasts (about 3), cut into approximately 1½-by-¼-by-¼-inch strips

1. In a large pot, heat 2 tablespoons of the oil over moderately high heat. Add the tortillas and cook, stirring frequently, until brown and crisp, 3 to 4 minutes. Remove the tortillas from the pot and drain on paper towels.

2. In a blender, combine the garlic, jalapeño, avocados, lime juice, Tabasco, 1½ cups of the water, ½ teaspoon of the salt, and the pepper. Puree until smooth.

3. Heat the remaining 1½ tablespoons oil in the pot over moderate heat. Add the onion and cook, stirring frequently, until translucent, about 5 minutes. Add the broth and the remaining 2 cups water and 1 teaspoon salt. Bring to a simmer. Stir the chicken into the pot; cook until just done, 2 to 3 minutes. Add the avocado puree. Heat through, about 2 minutes. Serve the soup topped with the crisp tortilla strips.

EVEN EASIER

Use broken-up **tortilla chips** in place of the fried tortilla strips.

CHICKEN AVGOLEMONO

The traditional Greek avgolemono soup is just chicken broth (thickened with egg and flavored with lemon) and rice. We add juicy bites of chicken breast and green peas to make the soup a meal.

WINE RECOMMENDATION
A wine really needs to be rich to hold its own with the egg thickener here, yet high enough in acidity to be refreshing. Though expensive, a Meursault, one of the great white Burgundies, will pair with the soup to make an experience you won't forget.

SERVES 4

1½ quarts canned low-sodium chicken broth or homemade stock

2 cups water

1½ teaspoons salt

1 pound boneless, skinless chicken breasts (about 3)

½ cup long-grain rice

3 eggs

3 tablespoons lemon juice

½ cup frozen peas, defrosted

1. In a large pot, bring the broth, water, and 1 teaspoon of the salt to a simmer. Add the chicken breasts to the pot and simmer until they are just done, about 10 minutes. Remove the chicken breasts from the pot; when they are are cool enough to handle, cut them into bite-size pieces.

2. Meanwhile, stir the rice into the simmering broth. Increase the heat and boil until the rice is almost tender, about 10 minutes. Reduce the heat to the lowest possible temperature.

3. In a medium glass or stainless-steel bowl, beat the eggs, lemon juice, and the remaining ½ teaspoon salt until frothy. Remove about 1 cup of the hot broth from the pot. Pour the hot liquid in a thin stream into the egg mixture, whisking constantly. Pour the mixture back into the pot and stir until the soup begins to thicken, about 3 minutes. Do not let the soup come to a simmer, or it may curdle. Return the chicken to the pot and stir in the peas.

VARIATION

Stir in three tablespoons of chopped fresh **dill** along with the peas.

MOROCCAN CHICKEN-AND-COUSCOUS SOUP

A mainstay in Morocco, steamed couscous topped with a very liquid stew is undeniably delectable, but not exactly quick. We've found, though, that combining all the ingredients in a soup yields similarly sumptuous results in a much shorter time. The dish is decidedly spicy; if you prefer less heat, just reduce the amount of cayenne.

WINE RECOMMENDATION
Soup with such a riot of flavors needs a wine that's big but simple. Try a California zinfandel here for its generous, spicy fruit, supple texture, and full body.

SERVES 4

2 tablespoons cooking oil

1 onion, chopped

1 pound boneless, skinless chicken thighs (about 4), cut into approximately 1½-by-¼-inch strips

¼ teaspoon cayenne

1 teaspoon ground cumin

1¾ teaspoons salt

¼ teaspoon fresh-ground black pepper

1 sweet potato (about ½ pound), peeled and cut into ¾-inch cubes

1 zucchini, quartered lengthwise and cut crosswise into 1-inch pieces

¾ cup tomato puree

1 quart water

2 cups canned low-sodium chicken broth or homemade stock

½ cup couscous

⅓ cup chopped fresh parsley

1. In a large pot, heat the oil over moderate heat. Add the onion and cook, stirring occasionally, until translucent, about 5 minutes.

2. Increase the heat to moderately high. Add the chicken, cayenne, cumin, salt, and pepper to the pot. Cook, stirring occasionally, for 2 minutes.

3. Stir in the sweet potato, zucchini, tomato puree, water, and broth. Bring to a boil. Reduce the heat and simmer, stirring occasionally, until the vegetables are tender, about 10 minutes.

4. Add the couscous to the soup. Simmer for 5 minutes, stirring occasionally. Remove the pot from the heat. Let the soup stand, covered, for 2 minutes; add the parsley and serve.

MULLIGATAWNY SOUP WITH CHICKEN

Probably the best-known example of Anglo-Indian cooking, mulligatawny (literally *pepper water* or *pepper broth*) is no more subject to a single definition than is minestrone. Despite its name, the soup is generally not incendiary.

WINE RECOMMENDATION

Gewürztraminer's litchi, apricot, and floral flavors are just perfect with the complex, sweet spices of Indian cooking. Go for a grand cru gewürztraminer from Alsace for enough oomph to match this soup.

SERVES 4

2	tablespoons cooking oil
1	onion, chopped
1	clove garlic, minced
½	teaspoon ground cumin
¼	teaspoon dry mustard
¼	teaspoon ground coriander
¼	teaspoon cayenne
⅛	teaspoon ground cloves
¼	teaspoon ground ginger
8	plum tomatoes, chopped
2	cups green or yellow split peas, rinsed
1½	quarts water
1½	teaspoons salt
4	boneless, skinless chicken breasts (about 1⅓ pounds in all)
¼	teaspoon black pepper
	Cilantro leaves, for garnish (optional)

1. In a large pot, heat the oil over moderately low heat. Add the onion, garlic, cumin, mustard, coriander, cayenne, cloves, and ginger and cook, stirring occasionally, until the onion is translucent, about 5 minutes. Stir in the tomatoes and cook for 5 minutes more.

2. Add the split peas, water, salt, and chicken breasts to the pot. Simmer, partially covered, until the chicken is just done, about 10 minutes. Remove the chicken breasts with a slotted spoon.

3. Continue simmering the soup, partially covered, stirring occasionally, until the split peas are tender, about 20 minutes. Shred the chicken and return it to the soup along with the black pepper. Serve the soup topped with cilantro leaves, if using.

OLD SPICE

Indian cooks prefer to use whole spices and grind them as needed. Commercially ground spices may not be quite the same, but they are quicker. Just remember that they do lose strength over time and are best used within a year of their purchase.

ESCAROLE SOUP WITH TURKEY MEATBALLS

They're not like Mama used to make: These succulent meatballs are formed from lean ground turkey instead of beef, and they're served in a light broth with escarole, not perched on top of spaghetti. (If you really miss that pasta, boil about a quarter pound of your favorite kind and stir it into the soup before serving.)

WINE RECOMMENDATION
Turkey is deceptively strong in flavor and can stand up to even the most powerful red wines. Here, try a raw-boned, rich petite sirah from California for a rollicking duet.

SERVES 4

1 pound ground turkey

2 eggs, beaten to mix

1 clove garlic, minced

1 small onion, minced

½ cup dry bread crumbs

½ cup grated Parmesan

½ cup chopped fresh parsley

1½ teaspoons salt

¼ teaspoon fresh-ground black pepper

3 tablespoons olive oil

½ head escarole (about ½ pound), leaves washed well and chopped (about 1 quart)

1½ quarts canned low-sodium chicken broth or homemade stock

2 cups water

2 tablespoons red- or white-wine vinegar

¼ teaspoon red-pepper flakes

1. In a medium bowl, mix together the turkey, eggs, garlic, onion, bread crumbs, Parmesan, parsley, ½ teaspoon of the salt, and the black pepper until thoroughly combined. Shape the mixture into twenty meatballs.

2. In a large frying pan, heat 1½ tablespoons of the oil over moderate heat. Add half the meatballs to the pan and cook, turning, until browned on all sides, about 3 minutes. Remove the meatballs from the pan and drain on paper towels. Repeat with the remaining 1½ tablespoons oil and the rest of the meatballs.

3. Put all of the meatballs, the escarole, broth, water, vinegar, red-pepper flakes, and the remaining 1 teaspoon of salt in a large pot. Cover and bring to a simmer over moderate heat, stirring occasionally. The meatballs should be cooked through by the time the broth comes to a simmer.

TURKEY, MUSHROOM, AND LENTIL SOUP

Turkey from the deli—or from last night's dinner—makes this hearty soup especially substantial. You can easily do without the meat, though; for a perfect vegetarian meal, the mushrooms and lentils can stand on their own.

WINE RECOMMENDATION

Zinfandel is the one truly American red, so why not serve it with our native bird? It's more than poetic license: Turkey's strong, gamy flavor, and the earthy lentils as well, requires a robust and fruity wine.

SERVES 4

2	tablespoons cooking oil
1	onion, chopped
10	ounces mushrooms, sliced thin
2	cloves garlic, minced
1	tablespoon soy sauce
1	cup lentils
1¾	teaspoons salt
2	quarts water
1	½-pound piece cooked turkey, cut into ½-inch cubes (about 2 cups)
¼	teaspoon fresh-ground black pepper
¼	cup plus 1½ tablespoons chopped fresh parsley

1. In a large pot, heat the oil over moderately low heat. Add the onion and cook, stirring occasionally, until translucent, about 5 minutes. Increase the heat to moderately high. Add the mushrooms and cook, stirring occasionally, until golden, about 5 minutes. Stir in the garlic and the soy sauce.

2. Add the lentils, salt, and water to the pot. Bring to a boil. Reduce the heat and simmer, partially covered, stirring occasionally, until the lentils are tender, 25 to 30 minutes.

3. Stir the turkey, pepper, and ¼ cup of the parsley into the soup. Top each serving with some of the remaining 1½ tablespoons parsley.

VARIATIONS

Try two cups of diced cooked **chicken** or **ham** instead of the turkey.

Pozole

Our version of this Mexican wonder is so quick to make that you may begrudge the extra time it takes to chop, dice, or slice the various garnishes. You can, in fact, do without them—or choose just a few.

WINE RECOMMENDATION
It's hard to pick a wine that would be at home with all the flavors and textures here. We'd opt instead for a crisp Mexican lager.

SERVES 4

2   tablespoons cooking oil

1   onion, chopped

1   pork tenderloin (about ¾ pound), cut into ½-inch cubes

2   cloves garlic, minced

3   cups water

3   cups canned low-sodium chicken broth or homemade stock

2⅔ cups drained and rinsed canned white hominy (two 15-ounce cans)

1¾ teaspoons salt

¼   teaspoon fresh-ground black pepper

Lime wedges, for serving

Garnishes such as diced avocado, cilantro leaves, chopped onion, shredded lettuce, thin-sliced radishes (optional)

1. In a large pot, heat the oil over moderate heat. Add the onion and cook, stirring occasionally, until translucent, about 5 minutes. Increase the heat to moderately high.

2. Add the pork to the pot and cook, stirring occasionally, until the pork starts to brown, about 3 minutes. Stir in the garlic, water, broth, hominy, salt, and pepper. Bring to a boil. Reduce the heat and simmer until the pork is just tender, about 10 minutes. Serve with the lime wedges and the other garnishes, if using.

Hominy

Hominy is dried white or yellow field corn with the hulls and germs removed. Often used in Mexican cooking, hominy (called *pozole* in Mexico) is available dried or canned. The dried version must be reconstituted, which takes several hours of simmering but fills your kitchen with an irresistible corn aroma. For speed, canned hominy is the delicious and easy choice.

VIETNAMESE PORK-AND-NOODLE SOUP

In many Asian cultures, long noodles symbolize long life. And in the spirit of that tradition, we've left the pasta whole here, to be eaten with chopsticks or even a fork. Of course, if you're feeling reckless, you can go ahead and break the noodles into smaller pieces before cooking them.

WINE RECOMMENDATION

More and more Asian fusion chefs are discovering how well riesling complements their food. Try a Mosel kabinett here to see how its sweetness balances the soup's salty flavors while the bright citrus flavors in both shine through.

SERVES 4

¼ pound linguine

1½ tablespoons cooking oil

1 pork tenderloin (about ¾ pound), cut into 1½-by-½-by-½-inch strips

6 scallions including green tops, chopped

1 tablespoon chopped fresh ginger

2 tomatoes, chopped

3 tablespoons Asian fish sauce (nam pla or nuoc mam)*

1 teaspoon salt

2 cups water

1 quart canned low-sodium chicken broth or homemade stock

¼ pound bean sprouts

2 tablespoons lime juice (from about 1 lime), plus lime wedges for serving

1 cucumber, peeled, halved lengthwise, seeded, and cut crosswise into thin slices

1 cup lightly packed mint, basil, or cilantro leaves, or a combination

*Available at Asian markets and most supermarkets

1. In a large pot of boiling, salted water, cook the linguine until just done, about 12 minutes. Drain the pasta. Rinse with cold water and drain thoroughly.

2. Meanwhile, in another large pot, heat the oil over moderate heat. Add the pork, scallions, and ginger and cook, stirring occasionally, for 2 minutes.

3. Add the tomatoes, fish sauce, salt, water, and broth. Bring to a boil. Reduce the heat and simmer until the pork is just done, about 10 minutes. Stir the cooked linguine, bean sprouts, and lime juice into the soup. Ladle into bowls, top each serving with some of the cucumber and herbs, and serve with the lime wedges.

PORK-AND-TOFU SOUP

To make this soup as close as possible to the source of our inspiration, a Korean tofu stew, you'd need to use one of the many types of Asian chile-garlic pastes; about a tablespoon will do. An easier alternative—and a delicious one, too—is the combination of cayenne, paprika, and plenty of garlic that we've used here.

WINE RECOMMENDATION
Riesling wines and Asian flavors are truly a match made in heaven. Pay attention, however, to the degree of heat in the food; the more fire, the sweeter the wine should be to cool the burn. Here, a spätlese, preferably from Germany's Pfalz, is in order.

SERVES 4

1   cup rice
2   tablespoons cooking oil
1   pound boneless pork chops, cut into approximately 1½-by-¼-by-¼-inch strips
3   scallions, white bulbs and green tops chopped and reserved separately
3   cloves garlic, minced
¼   teaspoon cayenne
½   teaspoon paprika
5   cups water
2   ribs celery, sliced thin
1   zucchini, cut into ½-inch dice
¾   teaspoon salt
4   teaspoons soy sauce
4   teaspoons Asian sesame oil
1   teaspoon white- or rice-wine vinegar
1   pound firm tofu, cut into ½-inch cubes
¼   teaspoon fresh-ground black pepper

1. Bring a medium pot of salted water to a boil. Stir in the rice and boil until just done, 10 to 12 minutes. Drain.

2. Meanwhile, in a large pot, heat the oil over moderately high heat. Add the pork, the scallion bulbs, the garlic, cayenne, and paprika and cook, stirring frequently, until the pork starts to brown, about 2 minutes.

3. Add the water, celery, zucchini, and salt. Bring to a boil. Reduce the heat and simmer, partially covered, until the vegetables and pork are tender, 15 to 20 minutes. Stir in the soy sauce, sesame oil, vinegar, tofu, and pepper and cook for 5 minutes more.

4. Stir the scallion tops into the soup. Put a mound of rice in the center of each of four bowls. Ladle the soup around the rice.

MINESTRONE WITH WHITE BEANS AND ITALIAN SAUSAGE

The Italian *minestra* refers to a variety of moderately thick soups. Minestrone is a hearty vegetable-filled minestra that often contains beans and sometimes pasta. We've omitted the pasta here but added some Italian sausage. With minestrone, it seems, there is no end to the delectable variations.

WINE RECOMMENDATION
It's only natural to partner this traditional Italian soup with a classic Italian red wine. Either a Tuscan Chianti or a dolcetto from the hills of Piedmont will be splendid.

SERVES 4

1 tablespoon olive oil

1 pound mild Italian sausage, casings removed

1 onion, chopped

1 carrot, chopped

1 rib celery, chopped

1 clove garlic, minced

½ teaspoon dried thyme

1 bay leaf

4 cups drained and rinsed canned white beans, preferably cannellini (from two 19-ounce cans)

10 cups water

1 cup canned diced tomatoes with their juice

2 teaspoons salt

1 teaspoon fresh-ground black pepper

⅔ pound spinach, stems removed and leaves washed well (about 1½ quarts)

Grated Parmesan, for serving

1. In a large pot, heat the oil over moderately high heat. Add the sausage and cook, stirring frequently, until browned, about 5 minutes. Remove the sausage with a slotted spoon.

2. Reduce the heat to moderate. Add the onion, carrot, celery, garlic, thyme, and bay leaf to the pot and cook, stirring occasionally, until the vegetables soften, about 10 minutes.

3. Meanwhile, combine 2 cups of the beans and 2 cups of the water in a blender and puree until smooth.

4. Add the tomatoes, the bean puree, the remaining 8 cups water, the salt, and the pepper to the pot. Bring to a boil, skimming any foam that rises to the surface. Stir in the sausage, the remaining 2 cups beans, and the spinach. Simmer until the spinach wilts, about 3 minutes. Serve the soup topped with grated Parmesan, and pass more Parmesan at the table.

SMOKED-SAUSAGE, CABBAGE, AND POTATO SOUP

Sausage is one of our favorite soup ingredients, but we're less fond of the grease slick it can leave floating on the surface. Our solution: Brown the sausage while the soup is simmering, and combine the two just before serving. No cooking time added, and much fat subtracted.

WINE RECOMMENDATION
Portugal, while justly renowned for its ports and Madeiras, is also a great source of excellent values in robust, dry red wines. The earthy, spicy richness of these reds is perfect for rustic fare such as this. Ask for one at your local wine shop.

SERVES 4

2 tablespoons cooking oil

1 onion, chopped

1¾ pounds green cabbage (about ½ head), shredded (about 1¾ quarts)

1 pound baking potatoes (about 2), peeled, halved lengthwise, and cut crosswise into ½-inch slices

1 quart water

2 cups canned low-sodium chicken broth or homemade stock

1 bay leaf

1½ teaspoons dried thyme

1½ teaspoons salt

¾ pound smoked sausage, such as kielbasa, quartered lengthwise and sliced thin crosswise

1. In a large pot, heat the oil over moderately low heat. Add the onion; cook, stirring occasionally, until translucent, about 5 minutes.

2. Add the cabbage, potatoes, water, broth, bay leaf, thyme, and salt to the pot. Bring to a boil. Reduce the heat and simmer, partially covered, stirring occasionally, until the cabbage and potatoes are tender, about 20 minutes.

3. Meanwhile, put a large nonstick frying pan over moderate heat. Add the sausage and cook, stirring occasionally, until browned, 2 to 3 minutes. Remove the sausage from the pan and drain on paper towels. Just before serving, remove the bay leaf from the soup and stir in the sausage.

VARIATION

In a separate pan, cook three quarters of a pound of **sausage** links, cut into slices, and stir them into the soup instead of the smoked sausage.

HUNGARIAN BEEF-AND-POTATO SOUP

Traditionally, this soup would be made with cubes of beef, but when you want a quick weeknight dinner, who can wait for meat to braise? We use ground beef instead. If you like your soup spicy, substitute hot paprika for some of the sweet paprika here.

WINE RECOMMENDATION
France's southern Rhône is one of the world's treasure troves of red-wine values. Seek out a sturdy, spicy Côtes-du-Rhône-Villages or, if you can find one, a Vacqueyras. Their roasted raspberry flavors will complement the soup well.

SERVES 4

- 1 pound ground beef
- 1 large onion, chopped
- 1 green bell pepper, chopped
- 2 tablespoons flour
- 1 pound boiling potatoes (about 3), peeled and cut into 1/2-inch cubes
- 2 tablespoons paprika
- 1/4 teaspoon cayenne
- 1 teaspoon dried marjoram
- 1 1/4 teaspoons caraway seeds
- 1 1/4 teaspoons salt
- 1 tablespoon tomato paste
- 3 cups canned low-sodium beef broth or homemade stock
- 3 cups water

1. Set a large pot over moderate heat. Add the ground beef and cook, stirring to break it up, until the meat is no longer pink, about 2 minutes.

2. Reduce the heat to moderately low. Add the onion and bell pepper and cook, stirring occasionally, until the vegetables start to soften, about 10 minutes. Stir in the flour. Cook, stirring, for 1 minute.

3. Add the potatoes, paprika, cayenne, marjoram, caraway seeds, salt, tomato paste, broth, and water. Bring to a boil. Reduce the heat and simmer until the potatoes are tender, about 10 minutes.

VARIATION

Use one cup of wide **egg noodles** instead of the potatoes. You'll only need to simmer the soup for about five minutes, since the noodles don't take quite as long to cook.

STEAK-AND-POTATO SOUP

The hardest part of this soup is slicing the steak into thin, thin slices—but you can skip that step if you buy a package of presliced "beef for stir-fry" from the supermarket or sliced beef for *bulgogi* from an Asian market.

WINE RECOMMENDATION
If the steak and potatoes were on your plate, a Napa Valley cabernet sauvignon would be the obvious choice. It's the perfect pick here as well, but stay with an easy-drinking, light-tannin version for the best match.

SERVES 4

- 3 tablespoons cooking oil
- 1 pound sirloin steak, cut into ⅛-inch thick slices about 1½ inches long and ¾-inch wide, or 1 pound presliced beef (see headnote)
- 1¼ teaspoons salt
- 1 large onion, chopped
- 1 pound baking potatoes (about 2), peeled and cut into 1-inch chunks
- ½ pound green beans, ends trimmed
- 2 cups water
- 1 quart canned low-sodium chicken-broth or homemade stock
- ¼ teaspoon fresh-ground black pepper
- 2 teaspoons Worcestershire sauce

1. In a large pot, heat 1 tablespoon of the oil over moderately high heat. Add half the steak and cook, stirring frequently, until well browned, about 2 minutes. Remove the steak with a slotted spoon. Repeat with another tablespoon of oil and the remaining steak. Remove the steak from the pot and toss all of the steak slices with ¼ teaspoon of the salt.

2. Reduce the heat to moderately low and add the remaining tablespoon of oil to the pot. Add the onion and cook, stirring occasionally, until translucent, about 5 minutes.

3. Add the potatoes, green beans, water, broth, the remaining 1 teaspoon salt, and the pepper to the pot. Bring to a boil, scraping the bottom of the pot with a spoon to dislodge any brown bits. Reduce the heat and simmer until the potatoes are tender, about 15 minutes. Return the steak and any juices to the soup and stir in the Worcestershire sauce.

TEST-KITCHEN TIP

Make sure the steak is well browned before removing it from the pot; those brown bits left on the bottom are essential for flavoring the broth.

BLACK-BEAN AND CORNED-BEEF SOUP

Used to be, you'd stop at the deli counter to get the makings for a sandwich to accompany your soup; now, you can pick up the makings of the soup itself. Thin-sliced corned beef—or ham or pastrami, for that matter—makes for tender meaty morsels in a soup and needs no cooking time at all.

WINE RECOMMENDATION
This hearty soup calls for an equally hearty wine. Look for Australia's unique cabernet sauvignon/shiraz blend, a red wine redolent of blackberries, cassis, herbs, and eucalyptus. Its full body and frank fruitiness are just what you want.

SERVES 4

2	tablespoons cooking oil
1	onion, chopped
2	carrots, diced
2	ribs celery, diced
1	red bell pepper, diced
1½	teaspoons salt
3	cups water
3	cups canned low-sodium chicken broth or homemade stock
2	cups drained and rinsed canned black beans (one 19-ounce can)
1	jalapeño pepper, seeds and ribs removed, minced
½	pound sliced deli corned beef, cut crosswise into thin strips
1½	tablespoons red- or white-wine vinegar
¼	cup chopped fresh parsley

1. In a large pot, heat the oil over moderate heat. Add the onion, carrots, celery, bell pepper, and ½ teaspoon of the salt and cook, stirring occasionally, until the vegetables start to soften, about 10 minutes.

2. Add the water, broth, and the remaining teaspoon of salt to the pot. Bring to a boil. Reduce the heat and simmer until the vegetables are tender, about 10 minutes. Stir the beans and jalapeño into the soup and simmer for 5 minutes more.

3. Remove the pot from the heat and stir in the corned beef, vinegar, and parsley.

TEST-KITCHEN TIP

If you make the soup ahead of time, wait to stir in the last three ingredients until you're ready to serve. Otherwise, the flavor of the corned beef will leach out into the broth, the vinegar will lose its bite, and the parsley will turn brown.

CHAPTER FOUR

Green Salads

SHRIMP-AND-BOSTON-LETTUCE SALAD WITH GARLIC, ANCHOVY, AND MINT DRESSING

The name of this salad sums it up—boiled shrimp, a gutsy dressing, and tender greens. Mild Boston lettuce wouldn't usually support such a bold dressing, but here it works.

WINE RECOMMENDATION
The refreshing flavor of this salad requires a similarly refreshing wine. For a nice, cool accompaniment, choose a light, herbal sauvignon blanc from Italy's Alto Adige or Collio regions.

SERVES 4

- 6 anchovy fillets
- 2 cloves garlic
  Grated zest of $\frac{1}{2}$ lemon
- 1 cup packed fresh mint leaves
- $\frac{1}{2}$ cup plus 1 tablespoon olive oil
- $\frac{1}{4}$ cup lemon juice (from about 1 lemon)
- $\frac{1}{2}$ teaspoon salt
- $\frac{1}{4}$ teaspoon fresh-ground black pepper
- 1 pound large shrimp, shelled
- 2 small heads Boston lettuce (about $\frac{1}{2}$ pound in all), torn into bite-size pieces (about $2\frac{1}{2}$ quarts)

1. In a blender, combine the anchovies, garlic, and lemon zest. Pulse to chop. Add the mint, oil, lemon juice, salt, and pepper and blend until smooth.

2. In a large pot of boiling, salted water, cook the shrimp until they just turn pink, 2 to 3 minutes. Drain the shrimp and transfer them to a medium glass or stainless-steel bowl. Toss the shrimp with half the dressing.

3. Put the lettuce in a large glass or stainless-steel bowl and toss with the remaining dressing. Put the greens on plates; top with the shrimp.

VARIATIONS

■ **Grill** the shrimp instead of boiling them. Large shrimp will need about three minutes per side.

■ Substitute large **sea scallops**, either grilled or sautéed, for the shrimp.

GRILLED SCALLOPS OVER MIXED-GREEN AND HERB SALAD

A stylish mix of leafy greens and fresh herbs is a lovely bed for plump grilled scallops. Mix and match the herbs to your liking; you could even use all parsley if you prefer. Just make sure you have a total of two cups.

WINE RECOMMENDATION
America's love affair with pinot grigio is based in part on the wine's versatility, which extends even to many-flavored salads such as this one. Crisp, with a subtle nuttiness and a round, soft, medium body, a pinot grigio from Friuli will also be a perfect partner for the scallops.

SERVES 4

- 1 pound sea scallops
- 1 tablespoon plus ½ cup olive oil
- ¾ teaspoon salt
- ½ teaspoon fresh-ground black pepper
- 4 teaspoons sherry vinegar or red- or white-wine vinegar
- ½ pound mixed salad greens (about 4 quarts)
- ¾ cup loosely packed basil leaves, torn in half
- ¾ cup loosely packed flat-leaf parsley leaves
- ½ cup loosely packed mint leaves
- ¼ cup chopped fresh chives or scallion tops
- 4 teaspoons drained capers

1. Light the grill or heat the broiler. Toss the scallops with the 1 tablespoon oil, ¼ teaspoon of the salt, and ¼ teaspoon of the pepper.

2. In a glass or stainless-steel bowl, whisk together the vinegar and the remaining ½ teaspoon salt and ¼ teaspoon pepper. Add the ½ cup oil slowly, whisking.

3. Grill or broil the scallops, turning once, until they just become opaque in the center, 2 to 3 minutes per side.

4. In a large glass or stainless-steel bowl, combine the mixed greens, basil, parsley, mint, and chives. Toss the salad with the dressing and put it on plates. Top the salad with the grilled scallops and the capers.

VARIATIONS

- Substitute grilled **shrimp** for the scallops.
- Flaked cooked **salmon** would also be delicious in place of the scallops.

CRAB-AND-AVOCADO SALAD WITH GINGER VINAIGRETTE

Creamy avocados plus delicate crabmeat plus a tart ginger-and-lemon vinaigrette equals one great salad. Substitute cooked shrimp or grilled scallops for the crab in the equation, if you like; the result will be just as delicious.

WINE RECOMMENDATION
Avocados are so rich it can be hard to find a wine to match. Opt for contrast instead by using a crisp Italian white wine such as Soave or Orvieto. Its fresh but neutral flavors will stand back and let the salad shine.

SERVES 4

2   teaspoons chopped fresh ginger
     Grated zest of ½ lemon
2   teaspoons lemon juice
1½   tablespoons white- or rice-wine vinegar
2   scallions including green tops, chopped
1   teaspoon soy sauce
½   teaspoon salt
⅓   cup cooking oil
¾   pound watercress, tough stems removed (about 2 quarts)
½   head romaine lettuce (about ¾ pound), cut crosswise into 1-inch strips (about 2 quarts)
2   ripe avocados, preferably Haas, diced
½   pound lump crabmeat, picked free of shell

1. In a blender, combine the ginger, lemon zest, lemon juice, vinegar, scallions, soy sauce, and ¼ teaspoon of the salt. Pulse to chop. Add the oil and puree until smooth.

2. In a large glass or stainless-steel bowl, combine the watercress, romaine, avocados, and the remaining ¼ teaspoon salt. Toss the salad with all but 3 tablespoons of the vinaigrette and mound the salad on plates.

3. Toss the crabmeat with the remaining vinaigrette. Spoon the dressed crabmeat over the salads.

TEST-KITCHEN TIP

Wait until you're ready to toss the salad before dicing the avocados. The acidity in the vinaigrette will keep them from turning brown.

SMOKED-TROUT SALAD WITH GOAT-CHEESE CROÛTES

You don't need to make a special trip to the fish shop for smoked trout. The fish counter at most grocery stores will have it, vacuum-packed like many brands of bacon. We used plain smoked trout fillets, but the black-peppercorn type would be good, too.

WINE RECOMMENDATION

France's Chavignol is world renowned for both its Sancerre, made from sauvignon blanc, and its mouthwatering goat cheese. It's no accident that they are splendid together. Try a Sancerre here for the same delicious effect.

SERVES 4

1½ tablespoons red- or white-wine vinegar

2 teaspoons Dijon mustard

¼ teaspoon salt

Fresh-ground black pepper

⅓ cup plus 1½ tablespoons olive oil

12 ½-inch-thick slices baguette

6 ounces goat cheese, cut into 12 slices

1 pound spinach, stems removed, leaves washed well and torn in half (about 2¼ quarts)

1 large head radicchio (about ¾ pound), leaves torn into bite-size pieces (about 2¼ quarts)

½ pound smoked trout fillets, skin removed, flesh flaked

1. In a large glass or stainless-steel bowl, whisk together the vinegar, Dijon mustard, salt, and ¼ teaspoon black pepper. Add the ⅓ cup oil slowly, whisking.

2. Heat the broiler. Put the baguette slices on a baking sheet and brush the tops with the remaining 1½ tablespoons oil. Broil until lightly browned, about 2 minutes. Remove the baking sheet from the oven. Turn the slices over and top each one with a slice of goat cheese. Broil until the cheese is soft and warm, about 2 minutes. Sprinkle a little pepper over each croûte.

3. Meanwhile, toss the spinach and radicchio into the dressing. Put the salad on plates. Top with the trout and the goat-cheese croûtes.

VARIATIONS

■ Use **romaine** lettuce instead of spinach.

■ Add a handful of **frisée** to the spinach and radicchio.

SEARED-TUNA AND RADISH SALAD WITH LEMON VINAIGRETTE

Preparing this salad is no trouble at all, but if you want it easier than easy, or you just don't like medium-rare fish, use canned tuna instead of the fresh steaks.

WINE RECOMMENDATION
Pinot noir works beautifully with meaty fish such as salmon, swordfish, and especially tuna. For this salad, pour one of the many excellent examples from Oregon, where pinot noirs have bright raspberry flavors and a refreshing, lively crispness.

SERVES 4

7 tablespoons olive oil

½ teaspoon salt

¾ teaspoon fresh-ground black pepper

1 pound tuna steaks (about ½ inch thick)

3 tablespoons lemon juice

1 small clove garlic, minced

2 heads Bibb lettuce (about 1 pound), torn into bite-size pieces (about 3 quarts)

10 radishes, halved lengthwise and sliced thin crosswise

1. In a large nonstick frying pan, heat 1 tablespoon of the oil over moderately high heat. Sprinkle ¼ teaspoon each of the salt and the pepper over the tuna. Cook the fish for 2 minutes. Turn and cook until done to your taste, 2 to 3 minutes longer for medium rare. Transfer the tuna to a carving board.

2. In a small glass or stainless-steel bowl, whisk together the lemon juice, garlic, and the remaining ¼ teaspoon salt and ½ teaspoon pepper. Add the remaining 6 tablespoons oil slowly, whisking.

3. Cut the tuna into ½-inch-thick slices. In a large glass or stainless-steel bowl, combine the lettuce and the radishes and toss with all but 2 tablespoons of the vinaigrette.

4. Put the salad on plates. Top with the tuna slices and drizzle the remaining vinaigrette over the top.

VARIATIONS

Substitute two six-ounce cans of drained **canned tuna** for the fresh tuna. Skip Step 1 completely and add the drained canned tuna along with the lettuce and radishes.

SALMON-AND-POTATO CAKES WITH MIXED GREENS

Salmon cakes are one of our favorite old-fashioned dishes. Here, they top mixed greens dressed with a mustard vinaigrette for a familiar yet fantastic salad.

WINE RECOMMENDATION
The full flavors of this salad can take on a chardonnay that would drown out other dishes. Select a bottle from California's Napa or Sonoma Valley for a memorable treat.

SERVES 4

¼ cup plus 3 tablespoons cooking oil

1½ pounds baking potatoes (about 3), peeled and sliced thin

1¼ teaspoons salt

1 onion, grated

1 pound skinless salmon fillets

1 teaspoon fresh-ground black pepper

1½ cups water

¼ cup heavy cream

4 scallions, white bulbs only, chopped

3 tablespoons chopped fresh dill

1 teaspoon Dijon mustard

1 tablespoon red- or white-wine vinegar

½ pound mixed salad greens (about 4 quarts)

1 lemon, cut into wedges (optional)

1. Brush the bottom of a large deep frying pan with 1 tablespoon of the oil. Put the potatoes in the pan and sprinkle with ½ teaspoon of the salt. Top with the onion and then the salmon. Sprinkle another ½ teaspoon of the salt and ¼ teaspoon of the pepper over the salmon. Add the water to the pan, cover, and bring to a boil. Reduce the heat and simmer until the salmon and potatoes are done, about 15 minutes.

2. Remove the salmon and flake. Drain the potatoes well and put in a medium bowl. Add the cream and mash, leaving the potatoes fairly chunky. Add the salmon, another ½ teaspoon of the pepper, the scallions, and 2 tablespoons of the dill. Form the mixture into eight cakes; they needn't be perfectly symmetrical or smooth.

3. Wipe out the frying pan. Add 1 tablespoon of the oil and heat over moderately high heat. Add half the salmon cakes to the pan and brown well on both sides, about 5 minutes in all. Drain on paper towels and repeat with another tablespoon oil and the remaining salmon cakes.

4. In a medium glass or stainless-steel bowl, whisk together the mustard, vinegar, and the remaining 1 tablespoon dill and ¼ teaspoon each salt and pepper. Add the remaining ¼ cup oil slowly, whisking. Add the greens, toss, and put on plates. Top each salad with two salmon cakes and a lemon wedge.

GRILLED-CHICKEN-AND-ASPARAGUS SALAD WITH PARSLEY PESTO

Parsley, garlic, lemon juice, and oil—that's all it takes to make an outstanding dressing. The secret is in using a *lot* of parsley. You'll be surprised how flavorful it is.

WINE RECOMMENDATION

Asparagus can be hard to pair with wine, but sauvignon blancs from New Zealand handle the vegetable well, partly because they taste a bit like asparagus themselves. In addition, they are crisp enough to stand up to the vinaigrette.

SERVES 4

1 pound boneless, skinless chicken breasts (about 3)

1/3 cup plus 2 1/2 tablespoons olive oil

Salt

Fresh-ground black pepper

1 pound asparagus, tough ends snapped off and discarded

1 clove garlic

2 tablespoons water

1 1/2 cups loosely packed parsley leaves

1 tablespoon lemon juice

3 heads Bibb lettuce (about 1 1/2 pounds in all), torn into bite size pieces (about 4 1/2 quarts)

1. Light the grill or heat the broiler. Coat the chicken breasts with 1 tablespoon of the oil and sprinkle with 1/4 teaspoon each of salt and pepper. Grill or broil the chicken for 5 minutes.

Turn and cook until just done, about 5 minutes more. When the chicken breasts are cool enough to handle, cut them into bite-size pieces.

2. Toss the asparagus spears with 1 1/2 tablespoons of the oil and 1/8 teaspoon each of salt and pepper. Grill or broil the asparagus, turning occasionally, until tender, about 10 minutes, depending on the width of the spears. Cut the spears into 2-inch lengths.

3. In a blender, combine the garlic, water, parsley, lemon juice, 1/2 teaspoon salt, and the remaining 1/3 cup oil. Puree until smooth, scraping down the side of the blender with a spatula as necessary.

4. In a large glass or stainless-steel bowl, toss the lettuce, chicken, and asparagus with half the vinaigrette. Put the salad on plates. Drizzle the remaining vinaigrette over the salads.

CHICKEN SALAD WITH CUCUMBER, RED PEPPER, AND HONEY-MUSTARD DRESSING

Starting with cooked chicken—leftovers, perhaps, or a store-bought rotisserie chicken—keeps the preparation time short. If you want just chicken salad with no greens, skip the lettuce; double the chicken, cucumber, bell pepper, onion, and tarragon; and toss them with the dressing.

WINE RECOMMENDATION

Very often, ripe rieslings from Germany's warm Pfalz region taste of tropical fruits, including mangoes. This, along with their racy acidity, relatively light body, and low alcohol, makes them delightful sidekicks for cool summer salads.

SERVES 4

2 tablespoons lime juice (from about 1 lime)

1 tablespoon mayonnaise

2 teaspoons honey mustard

½ teaspoon salt

¼ teaspoon fresh-ground black pepper

½ cup olive oil

2 cups diced cooked chicken

1 cucumber, peeled, halved lengthwise, seeded, and cut into ¼-inch dice

1 red bell pepper, cut into ¼-inch dice

2 tablespoons minced red onion

1 large mango, peeled and sliced (optional)

2 teaspoons chopped fresh tarragon, chives, or basil

½ pound mixed salad greens (about 4 quarts)

1. In a large glass or stainless-steel bowl, whisk together the lime juice, mayonnaise, mustard, salt, and black pepper. Add the oil slowly, whisking.

2. In a medium glass or stainless-steel bowl, toss the chicken, cucumber, bell pepper, onion, mango, and tarragon with half the dressing. Toss the greens into the remaining dressing. Put the greens on plates and top with the chicken salad.

CHOOSING MANGOES

The skin of a ripe mango is yellow and red, and its flesh yields to gentle pressure. If you purchase a mango that is underripe (green and firm), put it in a paper bag and keep it at room temperature to ripen. Once the mango is ripe, you can refrigerate it for a couple of days before using.

SAUTÉED-CHICKEN SALAD WITH SOY LIME VINAIGRETTE

We suggest you save a couple of tablespoons of the vinaigrette to drizzle over the cooked chicken. Even better, use this reserved vinaigrette to deglaze the pan, and then drizzle the syrupy remains over the chicken. Pure flavor.

WINE RECOMMENDATION

A spicy but crisp red wine will work well with this robust salad. For something a bit off-beat, look for a Sancerre rouge, made from pinot noir, or a pinot noir from Alsace.

SERVES 4

- 8 tablespoons cooking oil
- 4 6-inch corn tortillas, halved and cut crosswise into thin strips
- 1 teaspoon salt
- 1 pound boneless, skinless chicken breasts (about 3)
- ¼ teaspoon fresh-ground black pepper
- ½ teaspoon ground cumin
- 2 tablespoons lime juice (from about 1 lime)
- ⅛ teaspoon cayenne
- 1½ teaspoons soy sauce
- 1 head green leaf lettuce (about ¾ pound), torn into bite-size pieces (about 2½ quarts)
- 1½ cups quartered cherry tomatoes (about ½ pound)
- 1 lime, cut into wedges (optional)

1. In a large frying pan, heat 1 tablespoon of the oil over moderate heat. Add the tortilla strips and cook, stirring occasionally, until brown and crisp, 3 to 4 minutes. Remove the strips from the pan; drain on paper towels. Toss the hot tortilla strips with ¼ teaspoon of the salt.

2. In the same pan, heat 2 tablespoons of the oil over moderate heat. Season the chicken breasts with ¼ teaspoon of the salt, the black pepper, and the cumin and add to the pan. Cook until brown, about 5 minutes. Turn and cook until almost done, about 3 minutes more. Cover the pan, remove from the heat, and let steam for 5 minutes. Remove the chicken from the pan. When the chicken breasts are cool enough to handle, cut them into ¼-inch-thick slices.

3. Meanwhile, in a large glass or stainless-steel bowl, whisk together the lime juice, cayenne, soy sauce, and ¼ teaspoon of the salt. Add the remaining 5 tablespoons of oil slowly, whisking. Set aside 2 tablespoons of the vinaigrette.

4. Put the lettuce, the tomatoes, and the remaining ¼ teaspoon salt into the bowl with the vinaigrette and toss. Put the salad on plates. Top with the chicken. Drizzle the reserved vinaigrette over the chicken and sprinkle the tortilla strips over all. Serve with the lime wedges.

CHICKEN-AND-SPINACH SALAD WITH TOASTED-SESAME DRESSING

Sesame seeds thicken and flavor the dressing here, and they're also tossed with the chicken, so you're sure to taste them in every bite. Keep a close eye on the seeds while they're toasting; it doesn't take long for them to go from golden brown to burned.

WINE RECOMMENDATION

The herbal, grassy notes in sauvignon blanc make it well-suited to pairing with salads. Even better, its high acidity allows it to easily handle the tart orange juice in this dressing.

SERVES 4

¼ cup sesame seeds

1½ teaspoons red- or white-wine vinegar

2 teaspoons chopped fresh ginger

1 small clove garlic

1 tablespoon orange juice

1½ teaspoons Asian sesame oil

⅓ cup plus 1 tablespoon cooking oil

½ teaspoon salt

1 pound boneless, skinless chicken breasts (about 3)

¼ teaspoon fresh-ground black pepper

2 tablespoons water

2 pounds spinach, stems removed, leaves washed well (about 4½ quarts)

1 red bell pepper, cut into thin strips

1. Heat a large frying pan over moderate heat. Add the sesame seeds and cook, stirring frequently, until browned, 2 to 3 minutes. Remove the seeds from the pan immediately.

2. In a blender, combine the vinegar, ginger, garlic, orange juice, sesame oil, the ⅓ cup cooking oil, ¼ teaspoon of the salt, and 1 tablespoon of the toasted sesame seeds. Puree until smooth and leave the dressing in the blender.

3. In the frying pan, heat the remaining 1 tablespoon oil over moderate heat. Season the chicken breasts with the remaining ¼ teaspoon salt and the black pepper and add to the pan. Cook until brown, about 5 minutes. Turn and cook until almost done, about 3 minutes more. Cover the pan, remove from the heat, and let steam for 5 minutes. Remove the chicken from the pan. Set the pan over moderate heat and add the water. Cook, scraping the bottom of the pan to dislodge any brown bits, until reduced to 1 tablespoon. Transfer the liquid to the blender and pulse to combine. When the chicken breasts are cool enough to handle, cut them into bite-size pieces and toss with the remaining sesame seeds.

4. In a large bowl, toss the spinach with the red-pepper strips and the chicken. Serve the salad with the dressing spooned over the top.

CHICKEN SALAD WITH WALNUTS AND ROQUEFORT DRESSING

Try this chunky, quick-to-make Roquefort dressing, and you'll never even consider using bottled blue-cheese dressing again. Although we have sautéed the chicken here, you can cook it any way you like—grilled, broiled, or even leftover or store-bought-rotisserie chicken will be fine.

WINE RECOMMENDATION

The salty Roquefort cries out for a sweet wine to provide contrast—but Sauternes, Roquefort's classic cheese-course partner, is too sweet. Try instead a drier and much less expensive Côteaux du Layon from the Loire Valley.

SERVES 4

½ cup walnuts

6 tablespoons olive oil

1 pound boneless, skinless chicken breasts (about 3)

Salt

½ teaspoon fresh-ground black pepper

1½ tablespoons red- or white-wine vinegar

2 tablespoons sour cream

¼ pound Roquefort or other blue cheese, crumbled

1 head green leaf lettuce (about ½ pound), torn into bite-size pieces (about 1½ quarts)

2 heads radicchio (about 1 pound in all), torn into bite-size pieces (about 3 quarts)

1. In a large frying pan, toast the walnuts over moderately low heat, stirring frequently, until golden brown, about 5 minutes. Remove the nuts from the pan and chop them into fairly large pieces.

2. In the same pan, heat 1 tablespoon of the oil over moderate heat. Season the chicken breasts with ¼ teaspoon each salt and pepper and add them to the pan. Cook the chicken until brown, about 5 minutes. Turn and cook until almost done, about 3 minutes longer. Cover the pan, remove from the heat, and let steam for 5 minutes. Remove the chicken breasts from the pan. When they are cool enough to handle, cut the chicken breasts into bite-size pieces.

3. Meanwhile, in a glass or stainless-steel bowl, whisk together the vinegar, sour cream, ⅛ teaspoon salt, and the remaining ¼ teaspoon pepper. Add the remaining 5 tablespoons of oil slowly, whisking. Add the Roquefort and stir just to combine, leaving the dressing chunky.

4. In a large glass or stainless-steel bowl, toss the lettuce and the radicchio with half the dressing. Put the salad on plates. Top the salads with the chicken. Spoon the remaining dressing over the chicken and then sprinkle with the nuts.

Vietnamese Cabbage-and-Chicken Salad

If you're a dark-meat fan, try boneless chicken thighs here in place of the breasts. They're just as easy to prepare, and add even more flavor to the salad. Let them simmer for about ten minutes rather than five.

WINE RECOMMENDATION

German rieslings, so often shunned at the table because of their sweetness, can be a sublime match for Asian cuisine. That sweetness acts as a foil to both the heat and the saltiness of the dishes. For this Asian salad, go with a kabinett from Germany's Mosel-Saar-Ruwer region for best effect.

SERVES 4

1 pound boneless, skinless chicken breasts (about 3)

3 teaspoons salt

2 tablespoons Asian sesame oil

1/2 jalapeño pepper, seeds and ribs removed, sliced

1 1-inch piece fresh ginger

2 cups water

1 head green cabbage (about 2 1/2 pounds), shredded (about 2 1/2 quarts)

2 tablespoons cider vinegar

2 tablespoons Asian fish sauce (nam pla or nuoc mam)*

1 1/2 tablespoons lime juice

3 carrots, grated

3 radishes, grated

4 scallions including green tops, chopped

2 cups coarse-chopped mint, basil, cilantro, or dill, or a combination

1 tart apple, such as Granny Smith, cored and grated

*Available at Asian markets and most supermarkets

1. Rub the chicken breasts with 1 teaspoon of the salt and 1 tablespoon of the sesame oil. In a medium saucepan, combine the jalapeño, ginger, and water. Bring to a simmer, add the chicken, and cover the pan. Simmer for 5 minutes. Turn the heat off and let the chicken steam for 5 minutes. Remove the chicken breasts from the saucepan; when they are cool enough to handle, pull them into shreds.

2. Meanwhile, in a large glass or stainless-steel bowl, combine the cabbage with the vinegar, fish sauce, lime juice, and the remaining 2 teaspoons salt. Toss and let stand for 10 minutes.

3. Add the carrots, radishes, scallions, 1 1/2 cups of the herbs, and the apple to the cabbage mixture. Stir in the remaining 1 tablespoon sesame oil. Serve the salad topped with the chicken and the remaining 1/2 cup herbs.

SPINACH-AND-TURKEY SALAD WITH CUCUMBER-AND-FETA DRESSING

A new twist on a Greek salad: The feta's in the dressing. After adding the cheese to the blender or processor, just pulse a few times to combine the ingredients; you want the dressing to be slightly chunky. Serve the salad with warm buttered pita.

WINE RECOMMENDATION
Sauvignon blanc is one of the few wines that can negotiate the aggressive flavor of feta. Try a zippy Sancerre or Pouilly-Fumé. Made entirely from sauvignon blanc, these are among France's most versatile wines.

SERVES 4

1 cucumber, peeled, halved lengthwise, and seeded

1/3 cup plain yogurt

1/4 cup olive oil

1 tablespoon red- or white-wine vinegar

2 tablespoons chopped fresh dill

1/2 teaspoon salt

1/4 teaspoon fresh-ground black pepper

1/4 pound feta cheese, crumbled

1 1/2 pounds spinach, stems removed and leaves washed well (about 3 1/2 quarts)

1 1/2-pound piece cooked turkey, cut into approximately 1-by-1/4-by-1/4-inch strips

2 cups quartered cherry tomatoes (about 3/4 pound)

1. In a blender or food processor, combine 1 cucumber half, the yogurt, oil, vinegar, dill, 1/4 teaspoon of the salt, and the pepper. Blend or process until smooth. Chop the remaining cucumber and add to the blender or food processor along with the feta. Pulse once or twice just to combine.

2. In a large glass or stainless-steel bowl, combine the spinach, turkey, tomatoes, and the remaining 1/4 teaspoon salt. Toss the salad with the dressing.

VARIATIONS

■ Use chopped fresh **oregano** instead of dill.

■ Add half a cup of Greek **olives**.

■ If you can get ripe summer **tomatoes**, use them instead of the cherry tomatoes.

CURLY-ENDIVE SALAD WITH BACON AND POACHED EGGS

We find warm egg yolk cascading over curly leaves of endive to be a truly delectable sight. In fact, we wouldn't consider it unreasonable to serve two poached eggs per person rather than one. If they aren't your thing, though, substitute wedges of hard-cooked egg.

WINE RECOMMENDATION The great name of Chablis has been debased by oceans of jug wine misappropriating the appellation. Real Chablis is made from chardonnay and has tangy apple and pear flavors that will be spectacular with this salad.

SERVES 4

 4   cups ½-inch cubes good-quality white bread
 6   tablespoons olive oil
     Salt
     Fresh-ground black pepper
 ½   pound sliced bacon, cut crosswise into ½-inch strips
 2   small heads curly endive (about 1½ pounds in all), torn into bite-size pieces (about 5 quarts)
 3   tablespoons plus 1 teaspoon red- or white-wine vinegar
 4   eggs
 1   clove garlic, minced
 ½   teaspoon dried thyme

1. Put a large frying pan over moderate heat. Toss the bread cubes with 2 tablespoons of the oil and ¼ teaspoon each of salt and pepper. Put them in the pan and cook, stirring frequently, until crisp and brown, about 5 minutes. Remove the croutons from the pan.

2. Add the bacon to the pan and cook until crisp. Remove and drain. Put in a large glass or stainless-steel bowl with the endive. Pour off all but ¼ cup of the fat from the pan.

3. Fill a saucepan two-thirds full with water. Add the 1 teaspoon vinegar and bring to a boil. Break each egg into a cup or small bowl and slide one at a time into the water. Reduce the heat to a bare simmer. Poach the eggs until the whites are set but the yolks are still soft, about 3 minutes. Remove with a slotted spoon and drain on paper towels. Sprinkle with salt and pepper.

4. To the fat in the pan, add the remaining 4 tablespoons oil, the garlic, thyme, and ¼ teaspoon each of salt and pepper. Warm the dressing over moderately low heat, stirring occasionally, until the garlic barely starts to brown, about 2 minutes. Add the remaining 3 tablespoons vinegar and remove from the heat. Toss the dressing with the endive and bacon until the endive wilts slightly. Add the croutons and toss again. Put on plates. Top each salad with a warm egg.

Mixed Greens with Smoked Ham, Black-Eyed Peas, and Roasted-Red-Pepper Dressing

Roasting the red peppers and lacing them with balsamic vinegar gives an appealing touch of sweetness to the dressing; it's a real winner. Try it on its own over grilled chicken or shellfish.

■ WINE RECOMMENDATION

This salad needs a crisp and frankly fruity red to contrast its smoky flavors. Beaujolais, easy to find and easier to drink, is a perfect choice.

SERVES 4

- 1 red bell pepper
- 1 clove garlic, smashed
- 1 tablespoon balsamic vinegar
- ¼ cup olive oil
- ½ teaspoon salt
- ¼ teaspoon fresh-ground black pepper
- ½ pound mixed salad greens (about 4 quarts)
- 1 ¼-pound piece smoked ham, such as Black Forest, halved lengthwise and cut crosswise into thin strips
- ¾ cup drained and rinsed canned black-eyed peas (from one 15-ounce can)

1. Roast the pepper over a gas flame or grill or broil it, turning with tongs until charred all over, about 10 minutes. When the pepper is cool enough to handle, pull off the skin. Remove the stem, seeds, and ribs. Cut the pepper into pieces.

2. In a blender, combine the roasted pepper, the garlic, vinegar, oil, salt, and black pepper. Puree until smooth.

3. In a large bowl, combine the greens with the ham and black-eyed peas. Serve the salad with the dressing spooned over the top.

VARIATIONS

If you'd rather use **frozen black-eyed peas**, cook them according to the package directions, drain, and let cool before adding them to the salad. Or you could substitute **black beans** or **kidney beans**.

WATERCRESS, SALAMI, AND GOAT-CHEESE SALAD

Watercress is not the most commonly used salad green, but its peppery bite makes it one of the most delicious. Baking the croutons is certainly a no-fuss method, but you can sauté them over moderate heat if that seems easier for you.

WINE RECOMMENDATION
Italy's light, thirst-quenching Bardolino will make a super sipper with this salad. Almost more of a rosé than a red, Bardolino can be utterly charming when made by one of the Veneto's many small artisanal wineries.

SERVES 4

- 1   quart ½-inch cubes good-quality white bread
- 9   tablespoons olive oil
-     Salt
-     Fresh-ground black pepper
- 2   tablespoons red- or white-wine vinegar
- 1¼ pounds watercress, tough stems removed (about 3½ quarts)
- ¼   pound sliced salami, halved and cut crosswise into thin strips
- 6   ounces mild goat cheese

1. Heat the oven to 350°. Put the bread cubes on a baking sheet and toss them with 3 tablespoons of the oil and ⅛ teaspoon each salt and pepper. Bake, stirring the croutons occasionally, until they are crisp and brown, 10 to 15 minutes.

2. Meanwhile, in a large glass or stainless-steel bowl, whisk together the vinegar, ½ teaspoon salt, and ¼ teaspoon pepper. Add the remaining 6 tablespoons oil slowly, whisking.

3. Add the watercress and the salami to the dressing and toss to combine. Toss in the croutons. Put the salad on plates and crumble some of the goat cheese over each serving.

VARIATIONS

- Mix some **arugula** in with the watercress leaves; just be sure to have a total of about three-and-a-half quarts of greens.
- Use strips of **pepperoni** instead of salami.
- Add some chopped **tomato**.

CHOPPED ITALIAN SALAD

Antipasto ingredients are sliced and diced to make a fun, flexible chopped salad. We've thrown in our favorites, and so should you. Add the dressing ingredients to the bowl, too, and mix them when you toss the salad—it's the Italian way.

WINE RECOMMENDATION The Piedmontese drink more of their native barbera than they do any other wine because its crisp acidity and bright blackberry flavors are at home with so many dishes. Try a Barbera d'Alba with this salad and you may become a convert yourself.

SERVES 4

1 head romaine lettuce (about 1¼ pounds), cut into 1-inch squares (about 3 quarts)

¼ pound sliced pepperoni, chopped

⅓ cup drained sliced pimientos (one 4-ounce jar)

⅓ cup chopped red onion

1½ cups drained, rinsed, and chopped canned artichoke hearts (one 15-ounce can), or 1½ cups pitted and chopped green or black olives

3 tablespoons red- or white-wine vinegar

¼ cup olive oil

½ teaspoon salt

¼ teaspoon fresh-ground black pepper

½ cup grated Parmesan

1. In a large glass or stainless-steel bowl, combine the romaine, pepperoni, pimientos, onion, and the artichoke hearts or olives. Toss to combine.

2. Add the vinegar, oil, salt, pepper, and Parmesan to the bowl. Toss thoroughly to combine the ingredients.

VARIATIONS

■ Use chopped **salami** or **prosciutto** instead of the pepperoni.

■ Add some chopped **pepperoncini** to spice up the salad.

■ Try a cup of drained and rinsed canned **chickpeas** instead of the artichoke hearts.

■ Diced **provolone** cheese would make a nice addition.

■ Stir in about a third of a cup of thin-sliced **basil** leaves.

GRILLED-STEAK AND ARUGULA SALAD WITH MUSTARD CAPER VINAIGRETTE

No wimpy little salad here. Thick slices of steak top peppery greens with a boldly flavored dressing over all. It's entirely satisfying.

WINE RECOMMENDATION
The great red grape of Italy's Piedmont is the nebbiolo, the basis of Barolo and Barbaresco, two complex, powerful, expensive wines. Purchase instead a Nebbiolo delle Langhe for a more frugal, lighter, but equally delicious experience.

SERVES 4

1½   pounds sirloin steak, about 1 inch thick

6   tablespoons olive oil

Salt

Fresh-ground black pepper

1   pound arugula, leaves washed and torn in half (about 2½ quarts)

2   cups halved cherry tomatoes (about ¾ pound)

1½   teaspoons Dijon mustard

½   teaspoon anchovy paste

1   tablespoon red- or white-wine vinegar

2   tablespoons drained capers

1. Light the grill or heat the broiler. Coat the steak with 1 tablespoon of the oil. Sprinkle the steak with ½ teaspoon salt and ¼ teaspoon pepper. Grill or broil the steak for 5 minutes. Turn the meat and cook to your taste, about 5 minutes longer for medium rare. Transfer the steak to a carving board and leave to rest in a warm spot for 5 minutes.

2. Meanwhile, put the arugula on a platter or on individual plates. Top with the cherry tomatoes and sprinkle with ⅛ teaspoon salt.

3. In a medium glass or stainless-steel bowl, whisk together the mustard, anchovy paste, vinegar, capers, ¼ teaspoon salt, and ⅛ teaspoon pepper. Add the remaining 5 tablespoons oil slowly, whisking.

4. Slice the steak on the diagonal. Put the slices on top of the arugula and tomatoes and drizzle the vinaigrette over all.

VARIATIONS

Use two quarts of **watercress** or **spinach** leaves instead of the arugula.

ROAST-BEEF SALAD WITH CREAMY HORSERADISH DRESSING

We think the dressing for this meaty salad has just the right kick. Which is not to say you can't add even more horseradish if you're so inclined; drain it well, though, or the vinegar it's packed in will upset the balance of the dressing.

WINE RECOMMENDATION
Wine lovers revere merlot for its soft, supple texture and seductive plum and chocolate flavors. Versions from Washington State have an added earthy note that will marry well with this dish.

SERVES 4

⅓	cup mayonnaise
⅓	cup sour cream
3	tablespoons drained bottled horseradish
1	teaspoon red- or white-wine vinegar
¼	teaspoon fresh-ground black pepper
¾	teaspoon salt
1	large head escarole (about 1½ pounds), torn into bite-size pieces (about 4 quarts)
¼	pound mushrooms, sliced thin
1	small red onion, sliced thin
½	pound sliced roast beef, cut into approximately 1½-by-½-inch strips

1. In a medium glass or stainless-steel bowl, whisk together the mayonnaise, sour cream, horseradish, vinegar, pepper, and ½ teaspoon of the salt until smooth.

2. In a large bowl, toss the escarole with the mushrooms, onion, roast beef, the remaining ¼ teaspoon salt, and all but 2 tablespoons of the dressing. Serve the salad with the remaining dressing drizzled over the top.

VARIATIONS

■ Instead of the roast beef, use leftover flaked **cooked fish** (salmon or any medium-firm white-fleshed fish, like cod, would be good) or use **smoked fish** (such as trout or whitefish).

■ Add a cup of cooked **broccoli** florets.

■ Stir in a cup or two of halved **cherry tomatoes**.

Corned-Beef Salad with Thousand Island Dressing and Rye Croutons

You've probably eaten a sandwich with a salad inside; now try a salad with a sandwich inside. Strips of corned beef are tossed with lettuce and rye-bread croutons, then topped with Thousand Island dressing—the real old-fashioned kind with "islands" of pickle relish, hard-cooked egg, and chopped scallion.

WINE RECOMMENDATION
Since the trade embargo was lifted in 1991, South African wines have become readily available here. The country's unique pinotage, a red grape created by crossing pinot noir and cinsault, has rich red-berry flavors and a hint of earthiness.

SERVES 4

3 cups ¼-inch cubes rye bread

1½ tablespoons cooking oil

¾ teaspoon salt

½ teaspoon fresh-ground black pepper

½ cup mayonnaise

2 tablespoons ketchup

   Dash Worcestershire sauce

1 tablespoon pickle relish

1 hard-cooked egg, chopped

3 scallions, white bulbs and green tops chopped and reserved separately

1 head green leaf lettuce (about ¾ pound), torn into bite-size pieces (about 2½ quarts)

½ head iceberg lettuce (about 1 pound), torn into bite-size pieces (about 1½ quarts)

½ pound sliced corned beef, cut into ½-inch-wide strips

1. Heat the oven to 350°. Put the bread cubes on a baking sheet and toss them with the oil and ¼ teaspoon each of the salt and pepper. Bake, stirring occasionally, until the croutons are crisp and starting to brown, 5 to 10 minutes.

2. In a small bowl, whisk together the mayonnaise, ketchup, Worcestershire sauce, ¼ teaspoon of the salt, and the remaining ½ teaspoon pepper. Add the pickle relish, the egg, and the scallion bulbs and stir to combine.

3. In a large bowl, toss together the lettuces, scallion tops, and corned beef. Serve topped with the dressing and the croutons.

Variations

■ Instead of the corned beef, add strips of deli **pastrami**, **ham**, or **turkey**.

■ Use **romaine** instead of iceberg lettuce.

CHAPTER FIVE

Other Salads

"SICILIAN" RICE SALAD

All right, we confess, this recipe isn't really from Sicily—we just invented it ourselves. But there's no denying the southern Italian heritage of the ingredients, and, like much of the region's cooking, our "Sicilian" salad is bold in flavor.

WINE RECOMMENDATION
The wine scene on the sun-baked island of Sicily is dominated by a few large players, one of which is the firm of Regaleali. Their inexpensive rosé is a delight and an appropriate choice for this salad.

SERVES 4

1½ cups rice

¼ cup pine nuts

⅓ cup drained and chopped oil-packed sun-dried tomatoes

2 tablespoons drained capers

⅓ cup chopped red onion (about ½ small onion)

1 6-ounce can tuna, drained

1 2-ounce tin anchovy fillets, drained and minced

¼ cup olive oil

1 tablespoon lemon juice

2 tablespoons red- or white-wine vinegar

¾ teaspoon salt

½ teaspoon fresh-ground black pepper

¼ cup thin-sliced basil or mint leaves

1. Bring a medium pot of salted water to a boil. Stir in the rice and boil until just done, 10 to 12 minutes. Drain. Rinse with cold water and drain thoroughly. Put the rice in a large glass or stainless-steel bowl.

2. Meanwhile, in a small frying pan, toast the pine nuts over moderately low heat, stirring frequently, until golden brown, about 5 minutes. Or toast the pine nuts in a 350° oven for 5 to 10 minutes.

3. Stir the toasted pine nuts, the sun-dried tomatoes, capers, onion, tuna, and anchovies into the rice. Toss the rice salad with the oil, lemon juice, vinegar, salt, pepper, and basil.

VARIATIONS

■ If you'd like **more anchovy flavor**, use some of the oil from the anchovy tin in place of some of the olive oil.

■ Add a handful of chopped pitted green or black **olives**.

RICE SALAD WITH SMOKED SALMON AND CUCUMBER

Call it sushi in salad form. The overall effect is pretty close to that of the Japanese specialty, even though the rice is arborio (short-grain, but not sushi rice), the salmon is smoked (not raw), and the spicy kick comes from horseradish (not wasabi).

WINE RECOMMENDATION
Chenin blancs from Washington State or Oregon are usually off dry. Their touch of sweetness helps to offset the horseradish's bite, their high acidity contrasts with the oiliness of the salmon, and their full body gives them the weight to stand up to its strong flavor.

SERVES 4

1½ cups arborio or other short-grain rice
¾ teaspoon salt
2 teaspoons sugar
3 tablespoons rice-wine vinegar
 Grated zest of 1 lemon
2 cucumbers, peeled
2 tablespoons sesame seeds
1 tablespoon cooking oil
1 tablespoon drained bottled horseradish
1½ teaspoons Asian sesame oil
½ pound thin-sliced smoked salmon, cut crosswise into ½-inch strips
4 scallions, white bulbs only, minced

1. Bring a medium pot of salted water to a boil. Stir in the rice and cook until tender, 10 to 12 minutes. Drain the rice well and transfer it to a large glass or stainless-steel bowl. Add ¼ teaspoon of the salt, the sugar, vinegar, and lemon zest and fold in with a rubber spatula. Set aside to cool.

2. Meanwhile, using a vegetable peeler, shave lengthwise slices from the cucumbers; discard the seeds. Put the cucumber slices in a strainer set over a medium bowl and toss them with the remaining ½ teaspoon salt. Set aside for at least 10 minutes.

3. In a small frying pan, toast the sesame seeds over moderate heat, stirring frequently, until light brown, 2 to 3 minutes. Remove the seeds from the pan.

4. Add the cooking oil, horseradish, sesame oil, and half the smoked salmon to the cooled rice and fold gently to combine. Divide the rice mixture among four plates or put it on a large platter. Top with the remaining smoked salmon. Squeeze the cucumber slices to remove any excess liquid and then put them on the salads. Sprinkle with the toasted sesame seeds and the scallions.

CHICKEN-AND-RICE SALAD WITH PESTO YOGURT DRESSING

Dinner doesn't get much simpler than this: Boil some rice and toss it with pesto, yogurt, and rotisserie chicken from the supermarket. Leftover cooked chicken or turkey will work just fine, too.

WINE RECOMMENDATION
Both the dominant herbal flavor of the pesto and the yogurt's acidic tang suggest a sauvignon-blanc-based wine. Once again, look to the Loire, sauvignon's ancestral home, for an herbal, gassy, citrusy Sancerre or Pouilly-Fumé.

SERVES 4

1½   cups long-grain rice

¾   cup plain yogurt

½   cup store-bought or homemade pesto

½   teaspoon salt

¼   teaspoon fresh-ground black pepper

1   roasted chicken, bones and skin removed (about 1 pound meat), meat torn into bite-size pieces (about 3 cups)

1. Bring a medium pot of boiling, salted water to a boil. Stir in the rice and boil until just done, 10 to 12 minutes. Drain. Rinse with cold water and drain thoroughly.

2. In a large serving bowl, whisk together the yogurt, pesto, salt, and pepper. Add the chicken and the rice and toss to combine.

PESTO

Store-bought pesto is perfectly acceptable for this rice salad (that's what we used), but if you'd like to make it yourself, here's an easy, delicious version.

MAKES 1 CUP

2   cloves garlic, chopped

1½   cups packed fresh basil leaves

¾   teaspoon salt

½   cup olive oil

¼   cup pine nuts

½   cup grated Parmesan

1. In a blender or food processor, mince the garlic and basil with the salt.

2. With the machine on, add the olive oil in a thin stream. Continue running the machine until the mixture is smooth, scraping down the ingredients if necessary. Add the pine nuts and Parmesan and blend or process until the nuts are chopped.

FUSILLI WITH SPINACH AND SUN-DRIED-TOMATO PESTO

Our tomato pesto packs a wallop of flavor. Use it in this colorful pasta salad or toss it with hot pasta instead. You may also want to try the pesto on top of grilled chicken, lamb, or vegetables; as a sandwich spread; or mixed with cream cheese on a bagel.

WINE RECOMMENDATION

There are seven different subzones within the Chianti growing area, among them the famed Classico. The best choice for this pasta, however, would be a Chianti from Rufina, where the wines are crisper, with more vibrant fruitiness.

SERVES 4

3/4 cup pine nuts

15 drained oil-packed sun-dried tomatoes, 5 of them chopped

1/2 cup olive oil

1/3 cup water

1 1/4 teaspoons salt

1/2 teaspoon fresh-ground black pepper

1 pound fusilli

1/4 pound spinach leaves, shredded (about 2 cups)

1 cup halved cherry tomatoes (about 6 ounces)

1/4 cup grated Parmesan

1. In a small frying pan, toast the pine nuts over moderately low heat, stirring frequently, until golden brown, about 5 minutes; remove from the pan. Or toast the pine nuts in a 350° oven for 5 to 10 minutes.

2. In a blender or food processor, put 1/4 cup of the pine nuts, the whole sun-dried tomatoes, the oil, water, 1/2 teaspoon of the salt, and 1/4 teaspoon of the pepper. Puree until smooth.

3. Meanwhile, in a large pot of boiling, salted water, cook the fusilli until just done, about 13 minutes. Drain. Rinse with cold water and drain thoroughly.

4. In a large glass or stainless-steel bowl, toss the pasta with the remaining 1/2 cup toasted pine nuts, 3/4 teaspoon salt, and 1/4 teaspoon pepper, the pesto, the chopped sun-dried tomatoes, the spinach, cherry tomatoes, and Parmesan.

VARIATIONS

■ Use chopped **walnuts** instead of pine nuts.

■ Add half a cup of roughly chopped pitted black **olives** to the salad.

SHRIMP-AND-ORZO SALAD WITH GREEK FLAVORS

Don't dilute your dressing: Drain that pasta really well before tossing it with the other ingredients. Here, the orzo needs to sit in a colander for a few minutes to be sure it's sufficiently dry. Then, if you want to be especially careful, give it an extra chance to drain on paper towels.

WINE RECOMMENDATION
Pinot blanc shows up in many versions around the world and is always at home with food. Here you should look to northern Italy's Friuli or Alto Adige for pinot blancs with subtle fruitiness and fresh herbal accents.

SERVES 4

½ pound orzo (about 1 cup)

1 pound large shrimp, shelled and halved lengthwise

1 tablespoon lemon juice

1 tablespoon red- or white-wine vinegar

¼ teaspoon salt

¼ teaspoon fresh-ground black pepper

1 tablespoon chopped fresh oregano, or 1 teaspoon dried oregano

⅓ cup olive oil

4 scallions including green tops, chopped

½ cup pitted and chopped black olives, such as Kalamata

¼ pound feta, crumbled

1. In a large pot of boiling, salted water, cook the orzo until almost done, about 10 minutes.

Add the shrimp to the pot and cook, stirring occasionally, until both the shrimp and orzo are done, 2 to 3 minutes longer. Drain thoroughly.

2. In a large glass or stainless-steel bowl, whisk together the lemon juice, vinegar, salt, pepper, and oregano; add the oil slowly, whisking.

3. Add the orzo and shrimp, the scallions, olives, and feta to the dressing and toss. Serve warm or at room temperature.

VARIATIONS

■ Substitute chopped fresh **marjoram** or **dill** for the oregano.

■ Add some diced **cucumber** to the salad.

■ Toss in some chopped **tomatoes** or halved **cherry tomatoes**.

PASTA SHELLS WITH SHRIMP AND GARLICKY BREAD CRUMBS

Parmesan and a lemon anchovy dressing coat shells, shrimp, and curly endive for a pasta salad that's second cousin to a shrimp Caesar. Instead of big croutons, sautéed bread crumbs make a crisp topping.

WINE RECOMMENDATION
There's a reason pinot grigio is so popular: It goes well with multiple- and strong-flavored food such as this. Full-bodied, yet fresh and tart, pinot grigio works with salads; its soft apple and nut notes are perfect foils for garlic and Parmesan.

SERVES 4

2 tablespoons plus ½ cup olive oil

1½ cups fresh bread crumbs

2 cloves garlic, minced

Salt

Fresh-ground black pepper

¾ pound medium pasta shells

1 pound large shrimp, shelled and halved lengthwise

3 tablespoons lemon juice

1 teaspoon anchovy paste

¾ teaspoon Worcestershire sauce

3 ounces shredded curly endive (about 2½ cups)

⅓ cup plus 2 tablespoons grated Parmesan

1. In a medium nonstick frying pan, heat the 2 tablespoons oil over moderate heat. Add the bread crumbs, garlic, and ⅛ teaspoon each of salt and pepper and cook, stirring frequently, until golden, about 5 minutes.

2. In a large pot of boiling, salted water, cook the pasta shells until almost done, about 10 minutes. Add the shrimp to the pot and cook, stirring occasionally, until both the shrimp and the pasta shells are done, 2 to 3 minutes longer. Drain thoroughly.

3. In a large glass or stainless-steel bowl, whisk together the lemon juice, anchovy paste, Worcestershire sauce, and ¼ teaspoon each of salt and pepper. Add the remaining ½ cup oil slowly, whisking.

4. Add the pasta and shrimp, the curly endive, and the ⅓ cup Parmesan to the dressing and toss. Serve the salad warm or at room temperature, topped with the garlic bread crumbs and the remaining 2 tablespoons Parmesan.

PAELLA SALAD

We've based this salad very loosely on paella, the Spanish rice dish—and you can actually make it with rice if you like. Our choice, though, is orzo, the tiny rice-shaped pasta. The cooking instructions are the same whichever you choose.

WINE RECOMMENDATION
Paella's Iberian roots lead us to Spain for a red Ribera del Duero. The name, literally translated as the "slopes along the Duero River," describes an area that is now the source of some of Spain's greatest red wines. Ribera del Duero's wild-cherry, herb, and spice flavors will be superb with this salad.

SERVES 4

3½ tablespoons olive oil

 1 onion, chopped

 1 green bell pepper, chopped

1¼ teaspoons salt

 6 ounces dried chorizo or other firm spicy sausage such as pepperoni, quartered lengthwise and sliced thin crosswise

¼ teaspoon dried red-pepper flakes

 1 teaspoon paprika

 1 pound boneless, skinless chicken breasts (about 3), cut into ½-inch cubes

¼ teaspoon fresh-ground black pepper

½ pound orzo (about 1 cup)

 2 tablespoons lemon juice

 1 tomato, diced

½ cup chopped fresh parsley

1. In a large frying pan, heat 1½ tablespoons of the oil over moderately low heat. Add the onion, bell pepper, and ¼ teaspoon of the salt. Cook, stirring occasionally, until the vegetables start to soften, about 10 minutes.

2. Increase the heat to moderately high. Add the chorizo and cook, stirring occasionally, for 2 minutes. Stir in the red-pepper flakes, paprika, chicken, ½ teaspoon of the salt, and the black pepper and cook, stirring frequently, until the chicken is almost done, about 3 minutes. Cover the pan and remove from the heat. Steam the chicken for 2 minutes. Transfer the mixture to a large glass or stainless-steel bowl to cool.

3. Meanwhile, in a large pot of boiling, salted water, cook the orzo until done, about 12 minutes. Drain. Rinse with cold water and drain thoroughly.

4. Add the drained orzo to the chicken mixture. Toss with the lemon juice, the remaining 2 tablespoons oil and ½ teaspoon salt, the tomato, and the parsley.

THAI-STYLE BEEF SALAD OVER ANGEL-HAIR PASTA

Laab—ground beef seasoned with chiles, lime juice, fish sauce, and mint—is a traditional Thai meat salad eaten warm or at room temperature. We've added thin noodles to turn it into a pasta salad, but you can always eat the meat mixture by itself; just cut down on the fish sauce, or the beef may be too salty.

WINE RECOMMENDATION

This dish would be a real challenge for most wines. A rich, fairly sweet and malty dark beer, however, will make a splendid chaser.

SERVES 4

½ pound angel hair or other thin pasta

2 tablespoons cooking oil

3 tablespoons Asian sesame oil

½ cup sliced almonds

1 jalapeño pepper, seeds and ribs removed, minced

1 teaspoon minced fresh ginger

1½ pounds ground beef

1 teaspoon salt

¼ cup Asian fish sauce (nam pla or nuoc mam)*

4 scallions including green tops, chopped

1 cup coarsely chopped fresh mint

¼ cup lime juice (from about 2 limes), plus 1 lime, cut into wedges, for serving

*Available at Asian markets and most supermarkets

1. In a large pot of boiling, salted water, cook the pasta until just done, about 5 minutes. Drain, rinse with cold water, and drain thoroughly. Toss the pasta with 1 tablespoon of the cooking oil and 2 tablespoons of the sesame oil.

2. In a large frying pan, toast the almonds over moderately low heat, stirring frequently, until golden brown, about 5 minutes. Or toast the nuts in a 350° oven for 5 to 10 minutes. Remove the nuts from the pan and chop them.

3. In a large frying pan, heat the remaining tablespoon of cooking oil over moderately high heat. Add half the jalapeño, the ginger, beef, and salt. Cook the meat, stirring frequently, until brown and cooked through, about 10 minutes. Remove the pan from the heat and stir in the remaining tablespoon sesame oil, the fish sauce, scallions, mint, and lime juice.

4. Put the pasta on plates and top with the beef salad. Sprinkle with the remaining minced jalapeño and the chopped almonds and serve with the lime wedges.

Couscous Salad
with Turkey and Arugula

Sweet raisins, crunchy nuts, spicy arugula—this couscous salad boasts an interesting array of flavors and textures. We include strips of roasted or smoked turkey to make it a meal, but you can leave them out for a meatless salad.

WINE RECOMMENDATION
It may surprise you to learn that Germany and Austria make good red wines, racy with brilliantly pure berry flavors. Look for Germany's dornfelder or Austria's Zweigelt for a brisk change of pace.

SERVES 4

- 2 cups water
- 1 teaspoon salt
- 1⅓ cups couscous
- ⅓ cup raisins
- ⅓ cup walnuts
- ¼ cup lemon juice (from about 1 lemon)
- ½ teaspoon fresh-ground black pepper
- 6 tablespoons olive oil
- 2 carrots, grated
- 1 ½-pound piece cooked turkey, cut crosswise into thin strips
- 5 ounces arugula, tough stems removed, leaves washed and chopped (about 3 cups)

1. In a medium saucepan, bring the water and ½ teaspoon of the salt to a boil. Stir in the couscous and raisins. Cover, remove from the heat, and let stand for 5 minutes. Transfer the couscous and raisins to a large bowl to cool.

2. Meanwhile, in a small frying pan, toast the walnuts over moderately low heat, stirring frequently, until golden brown, about 5 minutes. Or toast the nuts in a 350° oven for 10 minutes. Remove the nuts from the pan and chop them.

3. In a large glass or stainless-steel bowl, whisk together the lemon juice, ¼ teaspoon of the salt, and the pepper. Add the oil slowly, whisking.

4. Toss the carrots, the toasted nuts, the turkey, the arugula, and the remaining ¼ teaspoon salt with the cooled couscous. Toss the salad into the dressing.

VARIATIONS

Substitute three cups of shredded **watercress** or **spinach** leaves for the arugula.

TUNISIAN COUSCOUS SALAD WITH GRILLED SAUSAGES

We like to use a combination of sweet and hot Italian sausages here for alternating bites of mild and spicy, but don't feel limited by our preferences. Use your own favorite, and grill, broil, or even sauté it—whatever seems easiest to you.

WINE RECOMMENDATION
Australian shiraz is an all-purpose red that marries particularly well with anything from the grill. It offers lots of ripe blackberry flavor, pepper nuances, and a soft, lush texture.

SERVES 4

5	tablespoons olive oil
2	cloves garlic, minced
1⅓	cups couscous
1	teaspoon ground cumin
¼	teaspoon cayenne
¾	teaspoon salt
1	cup tomato juice
1	cup water
1	pound mild or hot Italian sausages or a combination
1	tablespoon lemon juice
1	tomato, diced
½	cup chopped cilantro (optional)

1. In a large frying pan with a lid, heat 1 tablespoon of the oil over moderately low heat. Add the garlic, couscous, cumin, cayenne, and ½ teaspoon of the salt to the pan. Cook, stirring occasionally, until the couscous starts to brown, about 3 minutes. Stir in the tomato juice and water. Bring to a simmer. Cover, remove from the heat, and let stand 5 minutes. Transfer the couscous to a platter or a large glass or stainless-steel bowl to cool.

2. Meanwhile, light the grill or heat the broiler. Coat the sausages with ½ tablespoon of the oil. Grill or broil the sausages, turning occasionally, until completely cooked through, about 10 minutes. Remove from the heat. When the sausages are cool enough to handle, cut them into thin slices.

3. Toss the cooled couscous with the lemon juice, the remaining 3½ tablespoons oil and ¼ teaspoon salt, and the tomato. Top with the sliced sausages and the cilantro.

SARDINE AND POTATO SALAD WITH ROMESCO SAUCE

Even non-sardine-lovers will enjoy this excellent salad with its garlicky sauce. We think one can of sardines is just the right amount, but if you're a big fan of the little fish, go ahead and use two.

WINE RECOMMENDATION
Many California winemakers are dedicated to producing wines from grapes associated with France's Rhône Valley. Look for a rich, honeyed, full-bodied marsanne from one of these "Rhône Rangers" to partner this salad.

SERVES 4

1½   pounds boiling potatoes, peeled, halved lengthwise, and cut crosswise into ¼-inch-thick slices

2   red bell peppers, 1 cut into paper-thin strips

½   pound plum tomatoes, halved lengthwise

⅓   cup blanched almonds

1   clove garlic

1   teaspoon paprika

   Pinch cayenne

1½   teaspoons red- or white-wine vinegar

2   tablespoons olive oil

1   teaspoon salt

¼   teaspoon fresh-ground black pepper

1   4-ounce can boneless, skinless sardines, drained

⅓   cup chopped fresh parsley

1. Put the potatoes in a medium pot of salted water. Bring to a boil. Boil until the potato slices are barely tender, about 5 minutes. Drain the potatoes thoroughly.

2. Meanwhile, heat the broiler. Stand the whole bell pepper upright and cut the flesh from each of the sides, leaving the stem, seeds, and core behind. Put the pepper and the plum-tomato halves on an aluminum-foil-lined baking sheet, cut-side down. Broil until charred, about 5 minutes. Peel off and discard the blackened skin.

3. Put the roasted pepper and tomatoes in a food processor or blender. Add the almonds, garlic, paprika, cayenne, vinegar, oil, ¾ teaspoon of the salt, and the black pepper. Puree until almost smooth.

4. In a large glass or stainless-steel bowl, toss the sardines with the potatoes, the bell-pepper strips, and the remaining ¼ teaspoon salt. Toss the salad with 1 cup of the romesco sauce and sprinkle the parsley over the top. Pass the remaining romesco sauce at the table.

SALMON, FENNEL, AND POTATO SALAD WITH SOUR-CREAM DRESSING

Feathery fennel fronds give this creamy dressing an added bit of flavor, but if you should find yourself with a frond-less fennel bulb, substitute a tablespoon of chopped fresh dill—or do without the greenery altogether.

WINE RECOMMENDATION
In the Pacific Northwest, where salmon is king, its queen is pinot noir. The oiliness of the fish makes it strong enough to partner a light red, and the complex red-berry and spice notes of the pinot noir are an ideal foil for the flavor of the salmon.

SERVES 4

1   pound Yukon Gold or boiling potatoes (about 3), peeled and cut into eighths

1   cup frozen peas

1   pound skinless salmon fillets

1   fennel bulb, fronds reserved, bulb sliced into matchstick strips

½   cup sour cream

¼   cup mayonnaise

2   tablespoons chopped fresh chives or scallion tops

2   tablespoons olive oil

1   tablespoon lemon juice

½   teaspoon salt

¼   teaspoon fresh-ground black pepper

2   bunches watercress (about ¾ pound), tough stems removed (about 1½ quarts)

1. Bring a large pot of salted water to a boil. Add the potatoes and cook for 8 minutes. Stir in the peas and continue cooking until the potatoes are tender, about 2 minutes longer. Drain thoroughly.

2. Meanwhile, fill a large, deep frying pan with 3 inches of salted water. Bring to a simmer. Add the salmon and simmer until the fish is just cooked through, about 10 minutes. Transfer the salmon to paper towels to drain. Cut or flake the salmon into bite-size pieces.

3. Chop enough of the fennel fronds to make 1 tablespoon. In a medium glass or stainless-steel bowl, whisk together the sour cream, mayonnaise, chives, oil, lemon juice, chopped fennel fronds, salt, and pepper.

4. In a large bowl, toss the watercress with ¼ cup of the dressing and put the greens on plates. In the same bowl, gently toss the potatoes and peas, the salmon, and the sliced fennel with the remaining dressing. Top the watercress with the potato-and-salmon mixture.

WARM SAUSAGE-AND-POTATO SALAD

For this French-style potato salad, toss the warm potatoes with broth or wine so they absorb the flavor of the liquid. If you can get a delicious French garlic sausage, this would be a great place to use it.

WINE RECOMMENDATION
The French often serve a simple and straightforward, fresh and fruity Beaujolais with smoked sausage and potato salad. Who are we to argue?

SERVES 4

- 1 pound boiling potatoes (about 3), peeled, halved lengthwise, and cut crosswise into ¼-inch slices
- 3 tablespoons canned low-sodium chicken broth or homemade stock
- ½ teaspoon salt
- 2 teaspoons Dijon mustard
- 1½ teaspoons red- or white-wine vinegar
- ¼ teaspoon fresh-ground black pepper
- ⅓ cup olive oil
- ½ pound smoked sausage, such as kielbasa, quartered lengthwise and cut crosswise into ½-inch slices
- 2 tablespoons chopped fresh parsley
- 1 large head romaine lettuce, shredded (about 2 quarts)

1. Put the potatoes in a medium saucepan of salted water. Bring to a boil and cook until the potatoes are just tender, about 5 minutes. Drain the potatoes and put them in a glass or stainless-steel bowl. Add the chicken broth and ¼ teaspoon of the salt to the warm potatoes and toss gently.

2. Meanwhile, in a large glass or stainless-steel bowl, whisk together the mustard, vinegar, the remaining ¼ teaspoon salt, and the pepper. Add the oil slowly, whisking.

3. Put a large nonstick frying pan over moderate heat. Add the smoked sausage and cook, stirring occasionally, until the sausage is brown and warmed through, about 3 minutes. Remove the sausage and drain on paper towels.

4. Toss the potatoes with 2 tablespoons of the dressing and the parsley. Toss the romaine into the remaining dressing. Put the lettuce on plates and top with the potatoes and sausage.

SWEET-POTATO SALAD WITH HAM AND CURRIED ALMONDS

An unusual potato salad, this starts with the homegrown combination of sweet potatoes and ham, and then turns exotic with a sprinkling of curried almonds. We like to perch the whole affair atop a bed of red leaf lettuce, but you can always choose to serve the potato salad without the greens.

WINE RECOMMENDATION

The sweetness of the potatoes, the spice of the curry, and the saltiness of the ham all point toward gewürztraminer as the wine of choice. Try a not-too-dry example from Alsace or Washington State for a match made in heaven.

SERVES 4

2 pounds sweet potatoes (about 3 large), peeled and cut into ½-inch dice

⅔ cup plus 1 tablespoon olive oil

3 tablespoons sliced almonds

½ teaspoon curry powder

1 ½-pound piece smoked ham, such as Black Forest, diced

3 scallions including green tops, sliced thin

3 tablespoons cider vinegar or red- or white-wine vinegar

½ teaspoon salt

¼ teaspoon fresh-ground black pepper

1 head red leaf lettuce (about 1 pound), torn into bite-size pieces (about 3 quarts)

1. Bring a medium pot of salted water to a boil. Add the sweet potatoes and boil until just tender, 5 to 10 minutes. Drain the sweet potatoes and transfer them to a large glass or stainless-steel bowl.

2. In a small frying pan, heat the 1 tablespoon oil over moderate heat until it is hot but not smoking. Add the almonds and curry powder and cook, stirring frequently, until fragrant, 1 to 2 minutes. Transfer the nuts to the bowl with the sweet potatoes and add the ham and scallions.

3. In a large glass or stainless-steel bowl, whisk the vinegar, salt, and pepper. Add the remaining ⅔ cup oil slowly, whisking. Toss half the dressing into the sweet-potato mixture.

4. Toss the lettuce into the remaining dressing. Put on plates and top with the potato salad.

VARIATION

The curried nuts and ham make great complements to sweet potatoes, but they're excellent with regular **boiling potatoes**, too.

LENTIL SALAD WITH
SPINACH, PECANS, AND CHEDDAR

Spinach serves two purposes here: Half of the leaves are shredded and wilted with the warm lentils, while the rest is dressed and makes a base for the salad. For the cheese, choose a good-quality aged white or yellow cheddar; its sharp flavor will perfectly contrast the lentils' earthiness.

WINE RECOMMENDATION
This salad, with its lentils and rich cheddar, can easily stand up to a fruity red wine. A petite sirah's roasted-berry flavors make it just right for the part.

SERVES 4

1	pound lentils (about 2⅓ cups)
1	small onion, halved
1	carrot, halved
1	clove garlic
1	bay leaf
⅓	cup pecans
4	tablespoons red- or white-wine vinegar
1	teaspoon salt
½	teaspoon fresh-ground black pepper
½	cup olive oil
1½	pounds spinach, stems removed, leaves washed well (about 3½ quarts)
¼	pound aged cheddar cheese

1. In a medium pot, combine the lentils, onion, carrot, garlic, bay leaf, and enough water to cover by 2 inches. Bring to a boil. Reduce the heat and simmer, partially covered, until the lentils are tender, about 30 minutes. Drain; discard the onion, carrot, garlic, and bay leaf.

2. In a small frying pan, toast the pecans over moderately low heat, stirring frequently, until golden brown, about 5 minutes. Or toast them in a 350° oven for 5 to 10 minutes. Chop them.

3. In a large glass or stainless-steel bowl, whisk together 2 tablespoons of the vinegar, ½ teaspoon of the salt, and ¼ teaspoon of the pepper. Add the oil slowly, whisking.

4. Shred half the spinach and put in a large glass or stainless-steel bowl. Add the hot lentils and toss with half the dressing, the remaining 2 tablespoons vinegar, ½ teaspoon salt, and ¼ teaspoon pepper. Toss the mixture gently until the spinach wilts.

5. Toss the remaining spinach into the remaining dressing and put on plates. Top with the lentil mixture and the toasted pecans. Using a vegetable peeler, shave the cheese over the top.

Tuna-and-White-Bean Salad

Purists would insist on imported Italian canned tuna fish for this Tuscan classic, but we think plain old tuna from the supermarket is just fine, too. However, make sure the fish is packed in oil; not only will the tuna be infinitely more flavorful, we use the oil as part of the dressing.

WINE RECOMMENDATION

Vernaccia di San Gimignano, from the vineyards surrounding the oft-pictured hilltop town of San Gimignano, is a refreshing and racy wine. Its subtle almond flavors will blend well with the earthiness of the beans.

SERVES 4

2   6-ounce cans tuna packed in oil

3   cups drained and rinsed canned white beans, preferably cannellini (from two 15-ounce cans)

1   red onion, sliced thin

1   tablespoon drained capers

2   bunches watercress (about ¾ pound), tough stems removed and leaves chopped (about 2 quarts)

2   tablespoons olive oil

1   tablespoon red- or white-wine vinegar

¾   teaspoon salt

1   teaspoon fresh-ground black pepper

Put the tuna with its oil, the beans, onion, capers, watercress, olive oil, vinegar, salt, and pepper in a large bowl. Toss gently to combine.

Variations

- Use **arugula** instead of the watercress.
- Try canned **sardines** instead of the tuna.

Test-Kitchen Tips

- Since there are so few ingredients in this simple salad, you'll want to use really good canned beans; lower-quality beans are mushy. Among the many fine brands, we find Goya to be consistently reliable.

- If your tuna has less than one-and-a-half tablespoons of oil per can, add a little extra olive oil to make up the difference. We're counting on that much oil as part of the dressing.

SALADE NIÇOISE

Though it's justifiably famous, this Provençal specialty is hardly untouchable. Feel free to include any kind of vegetable you like. Radishes, blanched leeks, roasted peppers (or pimientos as in this recipe), marinated artichokes, and chickpeas are just a few of the additions we've enjoyed over the years. Lettuce is untraditional, too, but good; we've arranged our *salade niçoise* on a bed of romaine.

WINE RECOMMENDATION
For an elegant evening on the patio, why not pull out all the stops and enjoy a festive rosé champagne with this classic salad. Champagne's deceptively high acidity will contrast with the richness of the tuna while standing up to the dressing's vinegary tang.

SERVES 4

½ pound small red potatoes (about 4), or 1 large potato, quartered

¼ pound green beans, halved

2 tablespoons red- or white-wine vinegar

1 tablespoon Dijon mustard

½ teaspoon salt

½ teaspoon fresh-ground black pepper

½ cup olive oil

1 head romaine lettuce (about 1¼ pounds), torn into bite-size pieces (about 3 quarts)

4 hard-cooked eggs, peeled and quartered

1 2-ounce tin anchovy fillets, drained

2 tablespoons drained capers

1 6-ounce can tuna, drained

¼ cup drained diced pimientos (from a 4-ounce jar)

¼ cup pitted and chopped black olives, such as Niçoise or Kalamata

1. Put the potatoes in a medium saucepan of salted water and bring to a boil. Boil for 5 minutes and then stir in the beans. Continue boiling until the beans and potatoes are tender, about 5 minutes longer. Drain thoroughly. When the potatoes are cool enough to handle, peel them and cut them into quarters.

2. Meanwhile, in a glass or stainless-steel bowl, whisk together the vinegar, mustard, salt, and pepper. Add the oil slowly, whisking. In a large glass or stainless-steel bowl, toss the romaine with ¼ cup of the vinaigrette and then transfer to a platter or individual plates.

3. In the same bowl, toss the potatoes with 1 tablespoon of the vinaigrette and pile them on top of the romaine. Repeat with the green beans and the eggs, tossing each with 1 tablespoon of the vinaigrette and then arranging it on the romaine. Arrange the anchovies, capers, tuna, pimientos, and olives in piles on the lettuce. Pass any remaining vinaigrette at the table.

CHICKEN SALAD WITH CUMIN AND PARSLEY

All of our chicken salads make great quick dinners, atop a bed of lettuce as here or inside a sandwich. If you don't have any leftover cooked chicken and don't have time to cook, store-bought rotisserie chicken is just the thing.

WINE RECOMMENDATION
A sauvignon blanc from California, riper and with more melon and fig flavors than those from France, is what you want for a tasty match. A touch of oakiness helps, too. Wines labeled *Fumé Blanc* are more likely to be made in this style than those simply called sauvignon blanc.

SERVES 4

- 1½ tablespoons grated onion
- ½ cup mayonnaise
- ¼ cup plain yogurt
- ½ teaspoon ground cumin
- ¼ teaspoon salt
- ¼ teaspoon fresh-ground black pepper
- 3 cups diced cooked chicken
- ½ cup coarsely chopped fresh parsley
- 2 cups shredded lettuce, such as leaf lettuce or romaine

1. In a large bowl, whisk together the onion, mayonnaise, yogurt, cumin, salt, and pepper. Stir in the chicken and parsley and toss to combine.

2. Put the lettuce on plates. Top with the chicken salad.

MORE CHICKEN SALADS

YOGURT DILL CHICKEN SALAD

In a large bowl, combine 3 cups diced cooked chicken with 1 small minced onion, ⅔ cup plain yogurt, 1 tablespoon mayonnaise, 3 tablespoons chopped dill, ¼ teaspoon salt, and ⅛ teaspoon black pepper.

LEMONY FRUIT-AND-NUT CHICKEN SALAD

In a large bowl, combine 3 cups diced cooked chicken with 1 peeled, cored, and diced apple. Add 2 tablespoons raisins, ⅓ cup chopped toasted walnuts, 1 cup halved red seedless grapes, ½ cup mayonnaise, ¼ cup plain yogurt, 4 teaspoons lemon juice, and ⅛ teaspoon each salt and black pepper.

REALLY TERRIFIC GOOD-OL' AMERICAN CHICKEN SALAD

In a large bowl, combine 3 cups diced cooked chicken with 1 small minced onion, 2 ribs chopped celery, ¾ cup mayonnaise, and ¼ teaspoon each salt and black pepper.

PORK WITH MUSTARD LIME VINAIGRETTE

Cubes of just-roasted pork tenderloin fill in for braised beef in our version of a French salad of leftover beef and vinaigrette. We love it warm or at room temperature, but do be sure to let the salad stand for at least a few minutes before serving to give the pork time to soak up some of the delicious dressing.

WINE RECOMMENDATION
Merlot's soft, supple texture and ripe, juicy plum and chocolate flavors have made it a current favorite among red wines. Savor a well-made version from California's Napa Valley here, and you'll know what all the fuss is about.

SERVES 4

2 pork tenderloins, about ¾ pound each

1 tablespoon plus 1 teaspoon Dijon mustard

¼ cup plus 1½ teaspoons olive oil

¾ teaspoon salt

½ teaspoon fresh-ground black pepper

1 small red onion, cut into very thin slices

1 tablespoon lime juice

⅛ teaspoon dried red-pepper flakes (optional)

½ cup chopped cilantro or fresh parsley

1. Heat the oven to 450°. Coat the pork with the 1 tablespoon of mustard and the 1½ teaspoons of oil. Sprinkle it with ½ teaspoon of the salt and ¼ teaspoon of the black pepper. Put the pork on a baking sheet and roast until just done, 20 to 25 minutes. Transfer the pork to a carving board and leave to rest in a warm spot for 5 minutes.

2. Meanwhile, put the onion in a small bowl of cold water and let stand for 10 minutes. Drain the onion, rinse, and then pat dry with paper towels.

3. In a large glass or stainless-steel bowl, whisk together the lime juice, the 1 teaspoon mustard, and the remaining ¼ teaspoon each salt and black pepper. Add the ¼ cup oil slowly, whisking. While the pork is still warm, cut it into bite-size pieces. Add the pork, onion, red-pepper flakes, and cilantro to the vinaigrette and toss.

VARIATIONS

Leftover pork or beef would not only taste great, it would actually be more traditional. The meat should really be cooked through, though, not rare.

173

ALSATIAN HAM-AND-GRUYÈRE SALAD

In Strasbourg, the main city of the Alsace region in France, salads of meat or cheese tossed with onion and vinaigrette are popular snack fare. We use *both* meat and cheese to turn this snack into a meal. Just add some hearty bread.

WINE RECOMMENDATION
Alsace is known for its delicious white wines, but an excellent red, pinot d'Alsace, is made from pinot noir as well. It's worth looking for to create an intriguing regional pairing. If you can't find one, a fruity Beaujolais will do just fine.

SERVES 4

1 onion, cut into paper-thin slices

2½ teaspoons grainy Dijon mustard

2 teaspoons red- or white-wine vinegar

¼ teaspoon salt

¼ teaspoon fresh-ground black pepper

½ cup olive oil

1 pound sliced smoked ham, such as Black Forest, cut into matchstick strips

½ pound sliced Gruyère cheese, cut into matchstick strips

¾ cup chopped fresh parsley

1. Put the onion in a small bowl of cold water and let stand for 10 minutes. Drain the onion, rinse, and then pat dry with paper towels.

2. Meanwhile, in a large glass or stainless-steel bowl, whisk together the mustard, vinegar, salt, and pepper. Add the oil slowly, whisking.

Add the ham, cheese, onion, and parsley to the vinaigrette and toss.

VARIATIONS

This is a fine place to use cold cuts or left-over meat. Thin strips of **pork**, **lamb**, **beef**, **salami**, or **mortadella** could all be used in place of the ham. Or, for you meat lovers, try one of them in place of the cheese.

Planning Your Quick Meals

Look to this section for practical advice on deciding what ingredients to keep on hand and tips for how to make quick soups and a simple vinaigrette. You'll also find alternative uses for many of our salad dressings and a list of recipes in which you can include leftovers.

RECIPES PICTURED OPPOSITE: (top) pages 131, 25, 145; (center) pages 49, 169, 79; (bottom) pages 121, 99, 73

THE QUICK PANTRY

If you keep these basic staples on hand, you can make any recipe in this book with a minimum of shopping time. You'll only have to make one short stop to pick up whatever fresh produce, poultry, meat, or fish is necessary for the dish.

CUPBOARD

- anchovy fillets
- artichoke hearts, canned
- beans, canned: black beans, black-eyed peas, cannellini beans, chickpeas
- beef broth, low-sodium
- bread crumbs, dry
- chicken broth, low-sodium
- clam juice, bottled
- coconut milk, unsweetened
- couscous
- hominy, canned
- lentils
- mushrooms, dried
- oil: cooking, olive

- pasta, dried: various shapes
- pimientos
- raisins
- rice: arborio, long-grain
- sardines, canned boneless and skinless
- soy sauce
- split peas, green or yellow
- Tabasco sauce
- tomatoes: canned, juice, paste, sun-dried
- vinegar: balsamic, cider, red- or white-wine, rice, sherry
- Worcestershire sauce

SPICE SHELF

- bay leaves
- caraway seeds
- cayenne
- cinnamon, ground
- cloves, ground
- coriander, ground
- cumin, ground
- curry powder
- ginger, ground
- marjoram
- mustard, dry
- oregano
- paprika
- peppercorns, black
- red-pepper flakes
- rosemary
- sage
- sesame seeds
- tarragon
- thyme
- turmeric

REFRIGERATOR

- anchovy paste
- butter
- capers
- cheese: cheddar, feta, goat, Gruyère, Parmesan, Roquefort
- cream, heavy
- eggs
- fish sauce, Asian
- garlic
- ginger, fresh
- half-and-half
- horseradish, bottled
- jalapeño chiles
- ketchup
- lemons
- limes
- mayonnaise
- milk
- mustard: Dijon or grainy
- olives

- onions
- oranges
- parsley
- pesto
- pickle relish
- potatoes
- scallions
- sesame oil, Asian
- sour cream
- tortillas, corn
- yogurt, plain

FREEZER

- bacon
- nuts: almonds, cashews, pecans, pine nuts
- tortellini, cheese
- vegetables, frozen: black-eyed peas, green peas, spinach

IMPROVISING QUICK SOUPS

Soup-making is not a mystery. If you follow a few general steps, not only can you make any soup in this book, but you'll be able to improvise at will.

Heat   butter or oil in a pot large enough to accommodate all the ingredients.

Sauté   aromatic vegetables (such as chopped onion, celery, carrots, garlic, scallions) in the heated butter or oil until they're soft.

Stir   in any vegetables, meat, or poultry that need some time to cook, along with dried herbs, spices, and salt.

Add   broth, water, or other liquid to the pot and bring it to a boil. When the soup reaches a boil, reduce the heat and simmer until the ingredients are done. If you're serving the soup immediately, add raw pasta or rice after bringing the liquid to a boil, and cook until done.

Puree   the soup, if that's your intention. Return the soup to the pot.

Add   any ingredients that need to be cooked briefly (under five minutes) or just heated through, such as fish or shellfish, small pieces of raw chicken, deli meats, canned beans, precooked rice or pasta, and so on. If you're enriching the soup with cream, add it here.

Taste   the soup. Add more salt if needed and stir in any fresh herbs, fresh-ground pepper, citrus juice, or other appropriate flavor boosters.

Garnish   with additional fresh herbs, croutons, grated cheese, or other tasty treats.

Vinaigrette

Homemade vinaigrette is simplicity itself. It takes one minute to get a bottle of commercial dressing out of the refrigerator and shake it up. It takes two minutes to make this recipe. A basic vinaigrette is the dressing or at least the starting point of the dressings for the majority of the salads in this book. Here we give separate directions for this easy classic, with ideas for variations so you can develop your own house dressing.

MAKES 1 CUP

¼ cup red- or white-wine vinegar

1 teaspoon salt

¼ teaspoon fresh-ground pepper

1 teaspoon Dijon mustard

¾ cup oil

In a glass or stainless-steel bowl, whisk together the vinegar, salt, pepper, and mustard. Add the oil in a thin stream, whisking.

Make Ahead

Basic vinaigrette keeps perfectly in a closed container in the refrigerator for weeks. Just shake it and you're ready to go. Dressings with garlic or any kind of onion, however, begin to taste stale (in fact, much like bottled Italian dressing) after as short a time as overnight, and herbs turn gray. Make enough plain vinaigrette for a week or so and add the onion, garlic, or herbs directly to the salad before tossing.

Variations

■ Add a teaspoon or so of minced **shallot** or **scallion**, or half that quantity of **garlic**.

■ Shortly before serving, whisk in a tablespoon of fresh **parsley, thyme, tarragon, dill, cilantro,** or **any soft-leaved herb**, or a mixture of two or three.

■ A French vinaigrette is traditionally made with an oil that doesn't have too strong a flavor, such as peanut, but experiment with **any oil** you like.

■ Try **lemon or lime juice** or **balsamic or sherry vinegar**. Many people like a higher percentage of acidity than the traditional one part to three or four of oil. Adjust to your own taste.

■ You can add bottled ingredients that you have in the cupboard, such as **Tabasco, Worcestershire,** or **soy sauce**.

■ Embellish with **capers, olives, anchovy paste, poppy seeds, Parmesan, Roquefort,** grated **ginger** or **horseradish**; you name it.

MIX-AND-MATCH DRESSINGS

Many of the salad dressings in this book are so versatile, they'd be great tossed with other salads or warm vegetables, or even used as quick sauces for fish, chicken, or meat. Experiment with some of these winning combinations:

PAGE	DRESSING	TRY WITH
95	Garlic, Anchovy, and Mint Dressing	cauliflower, swordfish, tuna
99	Ginger Vinaigrette	shrimp, chicken, pork
103	Lemon Vinaigrette	broccoli, canned tuna, chicken
107	Parsley Pesto	carrots, roasted fish, veal chops
109	Honey Mustard Dressing	crab salad, grilled shrimp, pork
111	Soy Lime Vinaigrette	snow peas, steamed fish, pork
113	Toasted-Sesame Dressing	spinach, lentil salad, pork
115	Roquefort Dressing	potatoes, burgers, steak
119	Cucumber-and-Feta Dressing	tomatoes, chicken, lamb kebabs
121	Hot Bacon Dressing	spinach salad, green beans
123	Roasted-Red-Pepper Dressing	broccoli, fish and shellfish, chicken
129	Mustard Caper Vinaigrette	potato salad, tuna steaks, pork
131	Creamy Horseradish Dressing	beets, poached salmon, beef
133	Thousand Island Dressing	romaine, boiled shrimp, beef salad
141	Pesto Yogurt Dressing	zucchini, pasta salad, shrimp
143	Sun-Dried-Tomato Pesto	roasted vegetables, chicken, lamb
157	Romesco Sauce	shrimp, cod, chicken
159	Sour-Cream Dressing	baked potatoes, shrimp, chicken
173	Mustard Lime Vinaigrette	bean salad, corn on the cob, chicken

LEFTOVERS

Think of leftovers as a head start; they're the original time-savers. Listed here are the recipes in this book that use cooked poultry, meat, or fish—for which precooked ingredients would be fine. You might even plan to roast a little extra chicken or beef with Sunday's dinner to save yourself a step later in the week. We also list recipes to which you could add leftovers to make a slightly different dish. When adding leftovers to soups, stir them in at the last minute; you want them to reheat, not overcook.

Fish

Substitute leftover shellfish or finfish in:
- Asian Salmon-and-Rice Soup, *page 45*
- Green Gazpacho with Shrimp, *page 49*
- Corn-and-Crabmeat Soup, *page 55*
- Shrimp-and-Boston-Lettuce Salad with Garlic, Anchovy, and Mint Dressing, *page 95*
- Crab-and-Avocado Salad with Ginger Vinaigrette, *page 99*
- Salmon-and-Potato Cakes with Mixed Greens, *page 105*
- "Sicilian" Rice Salad, *page 137*
- Rice Salad with Smoked Salmon and Cucumber, *page 139*
- Shrimp-and-Orzo Salad with Greek Flavors, *page 145*
- Pasta Shells with Shrimp and Garlicky Bread Crumbs, *page 147*
- Salmon, Fennel, and Potato Salad with Sour-Cream Dressing, *page 159*
- Tuna-and-White-Bean Salad, *page 167*
- Salade Niçoise, *page 169*

Add leftover shellfish or finfish to:
- Creamy Asparagus Soup with Mushrooms and Gruyère Croûtes (crab would be especially nice), *page 21*
- Tomato Soup with Chickpeas and Pasta, *page 35*

Poultry

Substitute leftover cooked chicken or turkey in:
- Chicken Noodle Soup with Parsnips and Dill, *page 63*
- Chicken-and-Avocado Soup with Fried Tortillas, *page 65*
- Moroccan Chicken-and-Couscous Soup, *page 69*
- Turkey, Mushroom, and Lentil Soup, *page 75*
- Grilled-Chicken-and-Asparagus Salad with Parsley Pesto, *page 107*
- Chicken Salad with Cucumber, Red Pepper, and Honey Mustard Dressing, *page 109*
- Sautéed-Chicken Salad with Soy Lime Vinaigrette, *page 111*
- Chicken-and-Spinach Salad with Toasted-Sesame Dressing, *page 113*
- Chicken Salad with Walnuts and Roquefort Dressing, *page 115*
- Vietnamese Cabbage-and-Chicken Salad, *page 117*
- Spinach-and-Turkey Salad with Cucumber-and-Feta Dressing, *page 119*
- Chicken-and-Rice Salad with Pesto Yogurt Dressing, *page 141*
- Couscous Salad with Turkey and Arugula, *page 153*
- Chicken Salad with Cumin and Parsley, *page 171*

Add leftover chicken or turkey to:
- Tortellini and Spinach in Garlic Broth, *page 19*
- Fusilli with Spinach and Sun-Dried-Tomato Pesto, *page 143*
- Lentil Salad with Spinach, Pecans, and Cheddar, *page 165*

Pork

Substitute leftover pork roast or chops in:
- Cabbage-and-White-Bean Soup with Prosciutto, *page 39*
- Vietnamese Pork-and-Noodle Soup, *page 79*
- Pork with Mustard Lime Vinaigrette, *page 173*
- Alsatian Ham-and-Gruyère Salad, *page 175*

Add leftover pork roast or chops to:
- Indian Split-Pea and Vegetable Soup, *page 25*
- Black-Eyed-Pea Soup with Greens and Ham, *page 37*

Lamb

Substitute leftover roast lamb or chops in:
- Shrimp-and-Orzo Salad with Greek Flavors, *page 145*
- Couscous Salad with Turkey and Arugula, *page 153*
- Chicken Salad with Cumin and Parsley, *page 171*

Add leftover roast lamb or chops to:
- Chickpea and Lentil Soup, *page 31*
- Tomato Soup with Chickpeas and Pasta, *page 35*

Beef

Substitute leftover roast beef, steak, or braised beef in:
- Hungarian Beef-and-Potato Soup, *page 87*
- Black-Bean and Corned-Beef Soup, *page 91*
- Grilled-Steak and Arugula Salad with Mustard Caper Vinaigrette, *page 129*
- Roast-Beef Salad with Creamy Horseradish Dressing, *page 131*
- Corned-Beef Salad with Thousand Island Dressing and Rye Croutons, *page 133*
- Alsatian Ham-and-Gruyère Salad, *page 175*

Add leftover roast beef, steak, or braised beef to:
- Potato-and-Broccoli Soup, *page 23*
- Lentil and Linguine Soup, *page 29*

INDEX

Page numbers in **boldface** indicate photographs   ❦ indicates wine recommendations